"This book will prove utterly unforgettable."

"In *'O' God*, Dave Sterrett and Josh McDowell offer a work that is profoundly moving and surprisingly lighthearted. Through fresh fiction, they manage to deal carefully with the 'big issues' that often intimidate other spiritual writers. If you are in love with the daytime diva or are simply a spiritual seeker, this book will prove utterly unforgettable."

Merritt

for the

Southern Ba[   ]itiative

"In a culture offering myriad religious options, Dave Sterrett and Josh McDowell bring truth to light. *'O' God* creatively addresses the 'matters of the soul,' which most people long to explore. Spiritual seekers who are looking for answers will find God's truth as they ponder the words of this book. I recommend it as a guide and resource to help you sift through the variety of spiritual concepts presented through the media today."

—Karol Ladd
Author of *The Power of a Positive Woman*

" *'O' God* is a very readable conversation about Oprah's religious views—their popular appeal, their dangers, and their necessary theological and philosophical correctives. Given Oprah's remarkable influence, this book ought to be widely read."

—Dr. Paul Copan
Professor and Pledger Family Chair of Philosophy and Ethics, Palm Beach Atlantic University, and author of *When God Goes to Starbucks*

"Oprah is searching for ultimate meaning. *'O' God* is a fun read that will show you where Oprah has found the truth and where she should continue her search."

—Dr. Frank Turek
Author of *I Don't Have Enough Faith to Be an Atheist;*
Correct, Not Politically Correct; and *Legislating Morality*

"In a day and time when some people feel that truth becomes obscure and moral lines are blurry, *'O' God* addresses the popular concept of tolerance, along with other controversial ideas embraced and taught by Oprah herself, in a way that is easily accessible, scripturally based, and lovingly communicated. McDowell and Sterrett do a phenomenal job of comparing and contrasting Oprah's spiritual undertakings with God's Word and helping readers to thoroughly examine the spiritual trends of the day. Completely eye-opening and a must-read."

—Meredith Andrews
Recording Artist and Worship Leader

"Dave Sterrett possesses a remarkable gift for creatively communicating God's truth. As a popular speaker and well-trained theologian, Dave passionately tackles some of the toughest spiritual questions being asked by our generation. His skill as a writer and teacher make him an important new voice in the field of Christian apologetics. Read this book—you'll never be the same!"

—Marla Alupoaicei
Author of *Your Intercultural Marriage:*
A Guide to a Healthy, Happy Relationship

GOD

A Dialogue on Truth and
Oprah's Spirituality

JOSH McDOWELL
DAVE STERRETT

WND Books

"O" GOD

A WND Books book
Published by WorldNetDaily
Los Angeles, CA
Copyright © 2009 by Josh McDowell and David Sterrett

Jacket design and interior layout by Genesis Group, Bartlesville, OK

WND Books are distributed to the trade by:
Midpoint Trade Books
27 West 20th Street, Suite 1102
New York, NY 10011

WND Books are available at special discounts for bulk purchases. WND Books, Inc. also publishes books in electronic formats. For more information call (310) 961-4170 or visit www.wndbooks.com.

ISBN 13-Digit: 9781935071174
ISBN 10-Digit: 1935071173
E-Book ISBN 13-Digit: 9781935071716
E-Book ISBN 10-Digit: 1935071718
Library of Congress Control Number: 2009931568

Printed in the United States of America

10 9 8 7 6 5 4 3 2 1

Contents

Disclaimer
This book, including the title and cover, is not officially or unofficially connected with or endorsed by Oprah Winfrey, "The Oprah Winfrey Show," *O, The Oprah Magazine*, or any of her other associates or companies.

Acknowledgments

"O" God would never have been completed without the collaboration and encouragement of many friends. Shay Todd, thank you very much for helping put a creative and feminine touch on this entire manuscript. We also would like to show our appreciation to Bryce Taylor, Marla Alupoaicei, and Lynn Copeland for meticulously editing the entire book and for giving helpful suggestions. Professor Andrew Osborne and Dave's fellow students at the University of Dallas also provided good insights in Dave's creative writing course.

Many thanks to Clay Sterrett, Teresa Sterrett, Dr. William Sterrett, Adrienne Carpenter, Kerby Anderson, Catherine Anderson, Debbie Tindall, Jonathan Merritt, and John Wilson for reading the manuscript and offering literary, theological, or creative advice. Other people who need to be recognized for inspiring this work directly or indirectly through your writings include: Dr. Norman Geisler, Dr. Frank Turek, Dr. William Lane Craig, Dr. Gary Habermas, David Gregory, Dr. Paul Copan, Dinesh D'Souza, Ravi Zacharias, and Dr. J. Budziszewski.

Thank you, Daniel J. Bramzon and Graham Beckett, for editing and providing a legal review for WNDBooks.

And finally, thank you, Ami Naramor and Eric M. Jackson, for your publishing services and vision to release this work.

Preface

Even though sometimes the subject matter may get a little uncomfortable—and perhaps flat-out awkward—many people still love spiritual conversations. In some circles, there has been an increased interest in what some refer to as "interreligious dialogue." Women (and men) who have been influenced by Oprah Winfrey's spiritual teaching and endorsements of popular teachers like Marianne Williamson, Rhonda Byrne, and Eckhart Tolle are asking deeper questions about the nature of God, salvation, purpose, love, and Christ.

As Christian apologists who believe that salvation is by God's grace alone, through faith alone, and in Christ alone, we wanted to create a fictional, almost Socratic dialogue that would cover many of the themes of Oprah Winfrey's spiritual teaching in recent years. Our views are not necessarily purely represented by any of the characters in this fictional Socratic dialogue, nor do we claim that every single reference to Oprah by the characters is purely what she believes. Sometimes the characters disagree with their critique of Oprah. However, we do provide many exact quotations from Oprah and the books of her friends to make this spiritual interreligious dialogue as realistic as possible. Let us remind you that this story is fiction, but the story does contain many exact quotes from Oprah and her friends.

Even if you are not an Oprah fan, perhaps this story will encourage you in your own spiritual conversations. If you have a church community group or Sunday school class, we recommend that you use this book for discussion along with the

Scriptures. To help stimulate discussion, we have included sample questions in the back of this book.

You may wonder why we should talk about Oprah. Well, clearly she is a leader with influence and there's no doubt that people fed up with the traditional American church look to her as one of their spiritual leaders. In Cathy Lynn Grossman's *USA Today* article, "More Americans Dropping Dogma for Spirituality," she writes, "Religion today in the USA is a salad bar where people heap on upbeat beliefs they like and often leave the veggies—like strict doctrine—behind."[1] Quoting data provided from the Pew Forum on *Religion & Public Life's U.S. Religious Landscape Survey*, Grossman noted that 70 percent of all major Christian and non-Christian religious groups (except Mormons) say that "many religions can lead to eternal life."[2] And 68 percent say that "there's more than one true way to interpret the teachings of my religion."[3]

What we found especially interesting in this article was a quote from Rice University sociologist Dr. Michael Lindsay. Lindsay said, "Americans believe in everything. It's a spiritual salad bar. Rather than religious leaders setting the cultural agenda, today, it's Oprah Winfrey."[4] He continued, "After the attack on Pearl Harbor, the national memorial service was at Washington's National Cathedral, conducted by Episcopal clergy. After the 9/11 attack, Oprah organized the official memorial service at Yankee Stadium, and while clergy participated, she was the master of ceremonies."[5] He says, "The impact of Oprah is seen throughout this survey. She uses the language of the Bible and Christian traditions and yet includes other traditions to create a hodgepodge of personalized faith. Exclusivism (the belief that one religion has the absolute and exclusive truth) has gotten a bad name in America."[6]

If you are a Christ follower who believes, as we do, that God's salvation is only through Jesus Christ alone, perhaps this book, *"O" God*, will inspire a conversation with friends who are asking you questions. How do you respond when a friend at your work, school, book club, gym, or family reunion brings up Oprah Winfrey's teaching or a form of new spirituality? Do you know how to speak and live the truth in love? This book probably won't provide every single answer to all of your questions about God and spirituality, but we hope it will provide some. Our desire is that *"O" God* will create friendly and perhaps robust spiritual conversations about the most important things in your life.

CHAPTER 1

Watching "The Oprah Winfrey Show"

Isn't Oprah's spirituality influential?

Lindsey flopped down on the couch in her loft apartment, relieved to finally be able to enjoy a few moments of relaxation. Having just wrapped up the fall semester, she had only one semester of law school left at the University of Texas in Austin. She sighed. *I hope Christmas vacation will be relaxing*, she thought. She had received several prestigious job offers in both Austin and Dallas for the following year. She hoped the right job would bring her some emotional stability and relief from the stress of school.

But Dad won't be there. The shock of that thought resonated through her whole body. It was hard to believe he wouldn't be there to see her receive her law degree or start her new life. He had been so supportive of her dream to become a lawyer after her divorce, when she returned to graduate school at the age of thirty. But earlier in the year he had finally succumbed to the cancer he'd been fighting. She couldn't believe he was really gone.

Lindsey took her Subway sandwich out of the bag. She had just finished a yoga class at her gym. She flipped on the TV and was relieved to see that "Oprah" was on. In this intriguing rerun, Lindsey watched what seemed to be a hopeless dilemma in the lives of young children in a rural area of South Africa. Oprah said, "I visited classrooms with dirt floors and broken windows and met teachers who struggled to teach without pens, pencils, or paper."[7]

Oprah had recognized a dire need in that region of South Africa. She had witnessed a thousand children who came to school every day with no supplies but a passion to learn. Through Oprah's Angel Network, a new school was built and lives were changed.

Tears filled Lindsey's eyes. *She's so amazing!* Oprah had so much influence and wealth, yet she always used it to help others. Time and time again, Oprah found people who were hurting and made something happen to change their lives. *She's such a spiritual person.*

As the smiles of the beautiful children lit up the screen, Lindsey suddenly remembered the preacher she had seen on "Fox News" the previous night, who had said, "Oprah is the most dangerous woman in the world!"

How can these holier-than-thou Christians, like Reverend Judgmental and Mom's friends from Bible study, not appreciate Oprah? She always focuses on improving the lives of others, like these children... Sometimes Christians are just too hypocritical.

Lindsey took another bite of her turkey-and-cheese sandwich and then heard her phone vibrating. She glanced at it and saw that it was her friend Avatari. *Thank heavens there are a few exceptions.* She smiled at the thought. *I guess some Christians aren't so judgmental.*

Lindsey had met Avatari, her former yoga instructor, about two and half years earlier. "Your peaceful spirit got me through my divorce, my wretched thirtieth birthday, and my brutal first year of law school!" she had told her the first time she and Avatari went out for coffee. However, Avatari had stopped teaching yoga full time to focus on her Ph.D. studies in philosophy at the University of Texas. She taught a couple of Pilates classes and spent her Saturdays mentoring and tutoring young girls in an underprivileged community.

By her second year in the graduate Ph.D. program, Avatari, a former Hindu, had stopped teaching yoga altogether, but she continued to be a source of spiritual encouragement to Lindsey. *I still can't believe that Avatari became a Christian! And not just any old Christian—one who believes that the Bible is the freaking word of God! I don't get it. She's totally brilliant.*

Lindsey picked up the phone and punched the talk button. "Hey, girl!"

"How are you?" asked Avatari.

"Great! I just got back from yoga. What are you up to?"

"Studying, as usual."

"I'm watching an old 'Oprah' episode. You want to come over?"

"I'd love to, but..."

"I know...studying. I missed you today! Karen just doesn't have the same gift for teaching that you do. Sure wish you hadn't quit yoga. You're like an...an Indian goddess!"

Avatari laughed. "You are so full of it. But thanks. Have you talked with your mom? How is she?"

"She puts up a good front, but I know she's still lonely sometimes." Lindsey thought for a moment. "She misses Dad. It's about the time of the year when they would have taken their romantic anniversary trip to the Virgin Islands."

"I'm so sorry for her," said Avatari. "How are things for you, with Christmas coming up and all?"

Lindsey felt tears slipping from her eyes. "It's hard to talk about it. I miss Dad..." She tried to shake it off. "But thanks for all you've done for Mom and me, for the beautiful flowers and the food you brought over. She absolutely *loves* you. It's kind of funny—she still calls you Miss Universe."

"Oh, your mom is too sweet." Avatari hesitated for a moment. "That makes me think of Jack, for some reason."

"Sorry!"

"It's okay. I was just thinking that maybe if I really were Miss Universe, he wouldn't have left me for that other girl. But sorry. I shouldn't keep bringing his name up."

"Oprah has this incredible way of helping people. I mean, no matter what the problem is, she has answers. She certainly knows how to give people hope."

"You don't have to apologize. Don't tell yourself that! You're an amazing person, Avatari. You were way too good for him, and he knew it. You're gorgeous and brilliant. Every guy at UT is dying to date you."

Avatari laughed. "I don't know about that! But thanks, girl. You're so encouraging."

"Remember a couple months ago when both of us were really down on ourselves? We weren't in great shape, like when we ran our 10K together, but then we watched that 'Oprah' episode with the physical trainer guy, and we realized that we needed to start thinking positively—"

"—about *every* aspect of our being! Yeah, it was Bob Greene. I love that guy! He and Oprah definitely inspired us," said Avatari. "And it's true, real beauty goes so much deeper than whether we need to lose ten pounds. That was amazing—in just a few minutes watching 'Oprah' we changed our attitudes completely." ↓ *SHOWS HOW QUICKLY WE'RE INFLUENCED*

16

"She has this incredible way of helping people. I mean, no matter what the problem is, she has answers. She certainly knows how to give people hope." Lindsey paused. "Really, Avatari, you're a lot like Oprah. You're so positive, and you're really interested in the lives of others. Like the way you mentor and reach out to those young girls downtown. They really connect with you."

"Thanks, Lindsey. I never thought about that." Avatari sounded slightly embarrassed, but pleased.

"Hey, girl, are we still on for coffee on Tuesday?"

"Yep, eight thirty. Same place?"

"Sure. I still look forward to our conversations, even though you've gone and changed your beliefs on me. What am I going to do with you, now that you've become a Christian?" Lindsey asked jokingly. "You tick your father off because you won't marry anyone he chooses for you. Now you're constantly reading the Bible and all those theology books. Just promise that you'll never stop going out dancing with me. Or watching movies. Or having fun?"

Avatari laughed. "Nope. You have nothing to worry about. What makes you think I'd stop dancing? David danced half-naked, according to the Hebrew Scriptures. But don't worry, I won't get that extreme."

Lindsey laughed. "Okay, sorry. I shouldn't make fun of you. You know way more about that stuff than I do. Plus I'll have to start calling you 'doctor' pretty soon, so I shouldn't argue with you. I'll see you at coffee then?"

"Sounds great. Looking forward to it," laughed Avatari.

CHAPTER 2

Oprah.com

Is the God of the Bible a jealous God?

Lindsey woke abruptly from her nap. Sitting up in bed, she tried to shake off the grogginess. She hadn't meant to fall asleep, but studying until three in the morning the night before had taken its toll. She'd been dreaming that she and her dad were riding their bikes together around the lake like they used to do. The dream had felt so real. But as the dream fell away bit by bit and the darkness of reality crept in, Lindsey started to remember that her dad was really gone. An ache filled her heart.

God, are you there? Lindsey found herself thinking, surprising even herself. *If you're real, how could all of this happen to me? How could you allow my father to die? Wasn't the divorce I went through bad enough? Every relationship that I've been in has gone bad. Why don't any good Christian guys pursue me? Why do I always end up with jerks? Is it because I don't always know if I believe in you? Is it because I don't pray enough? Am I not a good enough person? By* this point, hot tears of anguish had started to stream down Lindsey's face.

Avatari is always so peaceful, God. She has something I don't. She's so sure of herself. She's so sure of . . . you. Please, God, if you're real—whoever or whatever you are—show me. Do you really love me? Are you even there at all?

Silent tears continued to fall after Lindsey prayed these words. Once they died away, she pulled out her Mac and went to Facebook. She saw that Avatari had posted a comment to her Facebook wall that immediately made her feel better. "Linds . . . your bridesmaid's photos at Beth's wedding look amazing! I can't wait to see you tomorrow for coffee. You are the best. I am praying for you and your wonderful mother."

Seeing that Avatari was online, Lindsey sent a message back: "Thanks for the message, Av! What are you up to?"

"Oh, you know, the life of a permanent graduate student. I'm studying as usual. Looking forward to seeing you tomorrow at Starbucks!" Avatari wrote.

Lindsey remembered something she'd wanted to tell her. "Hey, are you going to check out Oprah.com? She's interviewing Eckhart Tolle at seven. He's going to be talking about the book we're reading for Rachel's book club."

Lindsey minimized her Facebook window and went to Oprah.com. Within moments, history would be taking place. Lindsey hoped to take part in the largest spiritual conversation of all time, with millions of people from around the world joining an online interactive chat with Oprah Winfrey and Eckhart Tolle.

Lindsey's book group would be discussing Tolle's book *A New Earth* at Rachel's house on Wednesday night. *Hopefully, I'll get a head start and be able to contribute to the conversation with "Female-Socrates Avatari" and "Master-of-Divinity Rachel" on Wednesday.* Lindsey prided herself in being a bright litigator who had no problem tackling just about any issue. Discussing controversial topics had never bothered her. Even when she was growing up she made her youth pastor frustrated by asking tough spiritual questions. She was famous for stumping her Sunday school teachers with questions like:

- If God is all-good and all-powerful, then why is there so much evil?

- How do you know that the Bible hasn't been changed by people over two thousand years?

- What makes Jesus the only way to reach God?

Always up for exploring new ideas, Lindsey clicked on the link to spirituality. She began to listen as Oprah spoke to millions joined together online for the largest spiritual class in history. Oprah said:

> Welcome to our very first live, worldwide interactive event. We are here tonight breaking new ground. Nothing like this has ever been attempted before. Right now, you all are online with me from every corner on our planet. Places like Albania, Bolivia, Cambodia, Ecuador, Finland, Hong Kong, China, India, Zimbabwe, Australia, Canada, the UK, and the rest of Europe, along with all 50 states. Over 139 countries are represented in our class tonight. This is the most exciting thing that I have ever done. I've done a lot of things in my life. But I am most proud of the fact that all of you have joined me in this global community to discuss one of the most important subjects and one of the most important books of our time, *A New Earth*. We are going to be having a conversation from all around the world.[8]

For a few minutes, Lindsey sat and listened to Eckhart share about the importance of "getting in touch with the stillness within." He said, "I ask, 'What does life or God want from me?' and not just 'What do I want from life?'" Although Oprah preferred to use the word "God," Eckhart shared that he preferred the word "consciousness" to refer to the universal energy or ultimate metaphysical being.

Eckhart shared his personal experience of spiritual awakening. He observed that God (or the spirit of consciousness) flows through simple elements of nature, such as a flower, because those objects have less density than people do.

WHAT!

Next, Lindsey watched as Oprah fielded a question from an online participator named Kelly from Alton, Illinois. Kelly, experiencing the excitement of this historic event, said, "Thank you for having me. This is crazy!" She continued:

> My question is in regard to religion and spirituality. I had a Catholic upbringing. I married a Catholic and we're raising our children this way. Reading books such as Tolle's has really opened my eyes to a new way of thinking and a new form of spirituality that doesn't always align with the teaching of Christianity. Oprah, how do you reconcile these spiritual teachings with your Christian beliefs?[9]

Lindsey's ears perked up at Kelly's question. She'd been wondering the same thing. Oprah, sympathizing with the question and understanding that many other Christians shared this concern, said:

> I've reconciled it because I was able to open my mind about the absolute, indescribable hugeness of that which we call God. I took God out of the box because I grew up in the Baptist church and there were, you know, rules, belief systems indoctrinated. And I happened to be sitting in church in my late 20s. I was going to this church where you had to get out there at 8 o'clock in the morning to get a seat. Very charismatic minister. Everybody was into the sermon. And this great minister was preaching on how great God was and how omniscient and omnipresent and God is everything. And then he said that the Lord thy God is a *jealous*

God is jealous "for" me [handwritten margin note]

God. And I was, you know, caught up in the rapture of that moment until he is "jealous." And something struck me. I was thinking God is all, God is omnipresent, but God is *jealous?* God is jealous of me? And something about that didn't feel right in my spirit because I believe that God is love and that God is in all things. And so that's when the search for something more than doctrine started to stir within me.[10]

Lindsey understood why Oprah didn't feel right about God being jealous. That seemed contradictory to her idea that God was love. *I can see that,* she thought. *The jealous God described in the Old Testament seems a lot different from Jesus in the New Testament.*

From Eckhart Tolle's further comments, it became clear that although he seemed to have a positive view of Jesus, he believed that the Old Testament had a distorted view of God the Father. Lindsey remembered something Eckhart had written, that the God of the Old Testament is a patriarchal, controlling authority figure and an often angry man.[11] *not a man* [handwritten margin note]

Yeah, maybe the God of the Old Testament is really just a projection of the minds of religious extremists. Lindsey got caught up into the conversation, sympathizing with Oprah. *I agree with Oprah. I used to think the God of the Bible loved me, but after a while he started to sound like an angry God who only cared about rules and control. What was the deal with all of those rules? Pastor Chuck droned on and on about sex and alcohol. And the divorce... I know that a lot of narrow-minded Christians have judged me because of the failure of my marriage. They probably think that God was punishing me for something.*

Lindsey looked down and saw that Avatari was still online. *But Avatari is different,* Lindsey thought to herself. *I am not going to hold it against her for being a devout Christian. She studies lots of spiritual books, not just the Bible, and she knows so much. She's such a great person too. She really loves people and doesn't judge them. Maybe I just need to ask her if she believes God is jealous.*

Lindsey sent Avatari an instant message. "Did you see Oprah?"

"Part of it, but I was looking up something for my paper on Descartes."

"She said some interesting things. I've tried to consider some of these spiritual issues since Dad's death. I'm wondering again who God is, even though I thought I had slammed that door shut a long time ago. What do you think about God being jealous? Isn't it wrong to be jealous? Oprah talked about this. Did you see that part?"

Avatari sent a message back. "Yes, I saw it. Could jealousy ever be a good thing?"

"No, not really."

"Don't you think that God, as the infinite Creator of the entire universe, expects people to honor him most highly, *not* because he is insecure, but because he is all-knowing and all-loving and he knows what's best for us?"

"Well, I guess that's at least *possible*. But jealousy seems to conflict with love. And the Bible also says that God is love. Jealousy seems angry and controlling."

Avatari replied, "True. Oprah's pastor may have been referring to Exodus 34:14, which in some translations reads, 'Do not worship any other god, for the LORD, whose name is Jealous, is a jealous God.' But isn't jealousy sometimes combined with genuine love? In a marriage, a wife and husband expect each other to be faithful. When a husband leaves his wife for another woman, do you think that it's *wrong* for the wife to be jealous when she finds out about her husband's unfaithfulness? Isn't she justified in being jealous? Would her jealousy make her less good?"

"Okay, girl, speaking from experience, I can relate. No, I don't think being jealous would make her less good. That's natural. But why would God be jealous? He—or *she*—is God!" Lindsey wrote.

"Well, when we chase after material things and love those things more than God, I think God has the right to be jealous. It doesn't make him any less God. He knows that those false gods that we run after will only leave us empty and hurt."

Lindsey thought about some of her recent relationships. She had thought being with different guys would help her heal from the pain of divorcing Mark, but she only ended up feeling worse after each "pseudo romance" and each breakup.

"But God should be above that," Lindsey typed. "He shouldn't be emotional and wishy-washy like people are. It seems like people try to humanize him too much."

"Yes, but because the Bible was written by real people there are human descriptions of his nature. God inspired them to write, and they wrote books and letters containing a variety of literary styles: narrative, prophetic literature, laments, history, poetry, and more. Also, this term 'jealousy' isn't exactly the same as the jealousy that we experience. It's a figure of speech that gives human characteristics to God to help us finite humans understand him. The Bible describes God as a rock, a shepherd, a door, a bird, and a strong tower, but we know that God is not these things literally. Terms like this are used as analogies to help us understand God's character."

"When we chase after material things and love those things more than God, I think God has the right to be jealous. He knows that those false gods that we run after will only leave us empty and hurt."

"Hmm," Lindsey responded thoughtfully. "I never thought about that."

"Yeah, as human beings, our minds are limited to some extent. I'm pretty sure Oprah would agree. Lindsey, if God did inspire the Bible, wouldn't he want to use a language that would include figures of speech to help our limited minds understand?

I don't think that God's jealousy is the same as our self-centered jealousy. When I studied Hebrew, I discovered that the Hebrew word for jealous can also be translated as 'zealous' or 'passionate.'"

"But zealous and passionate make God sound too human and limited," commented Lindsey. "It sounds like some ancient fiction writer was just making up characteristics that he wanted God to have to try to control people."

"Well, just because God is infinite and all-powerful doesn't mean that he doesn't have feelings. I do, however, agree with you that his feelings aren't the result of actions imposed on him by others. His feelings flow from his eternal and unchangeable nature. God's passion is in correlation to the constant love that he feels for you."

Lindsey was surprised by Avatari's last statement. *His passion? Constant love? For me?* She paused to reflect.

God, could this be from you? she wondered. *I prayed that you would let me know if you're real, if you really love me. But this is Avatari. She loves everybody. Maybe she's just projecting her own message and saying that it's from you.*

Lindsey quickly typed back, "How so? If that verse says that God is jealous or passionate, how does that show his love?"

"God is *passionate* about having a relationship with you. The God of the Old Testament is the same as the God of the New Testament. Some of the finest biblical scholars who are experts in the original language translate that verse to say something like, 'You shall worship no other gods, but only the Lord because he is passionate about a relationship with you.' He's relational. He wants us to experience intimacy with him. He understands that nothing in this world will ultimately satisfy us: no material possession, no career success, no human relationship. He created these things to be good, but ultimately only he can satisfy. Lindsey, God knows what you have gone through with your ex and now with your dad. God loves you so much."

Lindsey was surprised by the depth of feeling in Avatari's response.

Avatari continued, "Since becoming a Christian, I've been studying the love of God throughout the Bible. I've discovered that God's love takes the initiative. Who would have thought that God would reveal himself to this Hindu philosophy student? You know that I used to believe in thousands of deities that were all connected, but God stepped in and got my attention. And my life changed. Now I know that the true God, through Jesus, was pursuing a loving relationship with me—just like he is with you. A verse that I discovered says, 'This is love: not that we loved God, but that he loved us and sent his Son as an atoning sacrifice for our sins.'[12] God knows everything about me. He knows everything about you. He knows what you are feeling. He understands you better than you understand yourself! His understanding of you is inexhaustible and boundless.[13] He even knows the number of hairs on your head.[14] Even the depths of your heart. And he still loves you with an indescribable love."

"But it's easy for you to believe, Avatari. I just don't feel it. I even tried praying a little while ago, but I'm not sure that anything happened. Why don't I *feel* like God is there? If God loves me, he should give me an experience that proves it. Then it would be so much easier for me to believe in him."

Avatari responded, "I understand. But true love is not always a feeling. Your feelings don't change the fact that God is passionate about a relationship with you. We won't *always* experience the feelings. You know there were times when you were little and your mom or dad asked you to do something that you didn't want to do. You didn't feel like their request was made out of love, but it was."

Lindsey thought back to her childhood introduction to God. *Maybe the God that my parents believed in really does exist. I used to believe in his love. I remember singing in Vacation Bible School,*

"Jesus loves me, this I know. For the Bible tells me so." But maybe I *was just a silly little kid being indoctrinated by legalistic Baptists. Maybe they just wanted me to "get saved."*

But then again, I know Avatari really believes in God, and God seems to love her and reward her for her faith in him. Lindsey sighed. *Is it true what Avatari is writing to me, or am I just so pathetic that I would believe anything at this point?*

Lindsey didn't know the answer. Her head spun with the lack of sleep and these confusing questions. *I'd better try to get at least a little bit more sleep before I have to wake up again,* she thought.

"Let's talk more at Starbucks. Is that cool?" she typed to Avatari.

"Sure. I'll see you in a few hours!" Avatari responded.

Lindsey got back into bed, pulled the sheet over herself, and willed herself to fall asleep. The questions would have to wait until morning.

CHAPTER 3

O, The Oprah Magazine

*Can't there possibly be more than
one way to heaven?*

H i! Welcome to Starbucks. What can we get started for you?"
asked the barista.

Hmm. I'm fifteen minutes early. Should I wait for Avatari?
Lindsey contemplated. *But I'm so thirsty. I guess I'll just go ahead
and order.*

"I'd like a tall skinny vanilla latte," responded Lindsey. "Oh,
and a bottle of water too, please. I'm parched from my spinning
class!"

"Sure, no problem," replied the barista.

As Lindsey waited for her drink order, she idly sifted through
the eclectic selection of CDs lying on a nearby rack: Jack Johnson,
Vintage Country, and Frank Sinatra. Then she spied someone's
copy of *O, The Oprah Magazine,*[15] apparently abandoned on a
small table in front of two plush, purple velvet chairs. Lindsey

sank down into a chair and glanced at the magazine cover, which featured a smiling picture of Oprah and these subtitles:

- Confrontation for Sissies—A Non-Scary Way to Say What You Need. *I don't think this is for me. Dad used to always tell me after our arguments, "You'll make a great lawyer."*

- How to Lose Weight after 40. *How about "how to lose weight at 32"? Even spinning class just doesn't seem to be getting the same results for me anymore, but the 22-year-olds at school make looking gorgeous seem effortless.*

- Beautiful Bottoms—At Last! Pants That Really Fit. *Well, maybe I'll check that one out. You can't really argue with that!*

Just then, the barista called out: "Tall skinny vanilla latte for Lindsey!" She stood up, grabbed the cup from the counter, and went back to check out the rest of the articles. She inhaled the relaxing aroma of the coffee and took a sip as she read the next title:

- Inside a Marriage—Confessions of a Semi-Happy Wife. *Hmm. Semi-happy. Maybe I should have read something like this before my divorce. If I could have found a way to be at least semi-happy, Mark and I could have stuck it out. But then again, he was a chauvinistic control freak who cheated on me. How could I have ever thought that he was my soul mate?*

Then Lindsey focused on the main title centered on the front cover:

HAVE YOUR OWN AHA MOMENT!
A practical guide to the spiritual side of life
Doubters welcome![16]

I could definitely use an "aha" moment—a real spiritual experience. It's been a while.

Just then, a memory from a long-ago church camp flashed through her mind.

She was sixteen, sitting on a log in front of a blazing campfire with about a hundred students from her church. Some went to her school and some were friends of friends, but over the course of the week, they had all gotten to know each other pretty well.

Brad, the youth pastor, had just finished giving a talk on how everyone needed to start being real and get right with God. The group had been sitting in quiet reflection for quite a while. The only sound was Greg strumming a worship song softly on his guitar. Brad had encouraged anybody who needed to get right with God to take a stand.

"I have something to say," said Travis as he stood up slowly, fidgeting with the cuff of his sweatshirt. *Wow, he's so hot!* Lindsey thought. *Emily is the luckiest girl in the world to get to go out with him.* "I know some of you look up to me as the captain of our football team, but I need to be honest tonight about who I really am. I need to get right with God. I've slept with lots of girls, and lately I've also been messing around with weed and some other stuff. And sometimes I watch movies that I shouldn't be watching..."

For some reason, Travis's confession really stirred the young people gathered there, including Lindsey.

Yeah, I was crying that night, and I really felt the presence of the Holy Spirit, Lindsey thought. *But maybe that was just emotion or manipulation from our youth pastor. We sang the same worship songs for hours until somebody started confessing their sin. The youth leaders seemed so excited about Travis's confession and his experience with Jesus. But the next weekend came around and he was getting high on weed and sleeping around again. Anyway, Oprah's spirituality makes a lot more sense. It seems deeper... it seems to offer the kind of freedom that I want.*

Flipping through a few pages, Lindsey stopped at a picture of Oprah that featured her letter of introduction to the magazine. Oprah began:

> It was Socrates who said that the unexamined life is not worth living, and I couldn't agree more. But I've also heard it said that the unlived life isn't particularly worth examining. So the question is, how do we live a life that's rich in substance and beauty, passion and meaning? This month we're delving into a subject that is dear to my heart and vital to my well-being: spirituality.[17]

Turning to the section on spirituality, Lindsey discovered an article by Martha Sherrill. She wrote:

> Whenever I visit my cousins in California, where I grew up, I'm reminded what a spiritually adventurous group we are. There are a dozen or more of us spanning the baby boomer generation. We span the spiritual landscape too. Having come from Christian grandparents—Catholic and various Protestant traditions—we are now all over the map. As my sister Anina says, "You know me. I'll look under any rock. And there isn't a spiritual practice that I won't try." We read Psalms and Thich Nhat Hanh. We've powered through C. S. Lewis and *Be Here Now.* We've done seminars in Lifespring, the Landmark Forum, and Transcendental Meditation. While a couple of my cousins were drawn to the Book of Mormon, and another joined a mainstream Protestant denomination, most of us wandered into the ancient Eastern traditions like Buddhism and Sufism.[18]

Sherrill continued:

> I used to feel embarrassed by our spiritual experimentation; it felt so hapless, so random. But on reflection, our explorations aren't so random after all; they're linked by a

unity of purpose, a common goal, which for lack of a better word I call authenticity.[19] *IF YOU ARE ALL OVER THE PLACE HOW IS THAT AUTHENTIC?*

In closing, the author asked:

> Is it really about the mat? This is where many Americans find themselves now, having moved beyond yoga "exercises" to a hunger for the prayers and practices underlying the poses. The goal is something we can't buy: spiritual maturation. We want to feel we're on the road to becoming fully developed spiritual beings whose lives are governed by wisdom, compassion, and a sense of acceptance. So we're browsing the spiritual marketplace, dropping new ideas and philosophies into our carts—a smidgen of Buddhism, some New Testament, maybe a little tai chi tossed in.[20]

Lindsey's mind started drifting to the similarities of what she heard Oprah say the night before: "Well, I am a Christian who believes that there are certainly more paths to God other than Christianity."[21]

"Hey, Linds!"

Lindsey looked up and saw Avatari walking toward her.

"It's so good to see you!" Lindsey replied and gave her friend a hug. "Let me get you something to drink."

"Oh, thanks, but you just sit right there and I'll be right back."

"What can I get for you?" asked the guy behind the counter.

"Can I please have a tall, no whip, cinnamon dolce latte?" Avatari replied. She looked over to where Lindsey was reading and noticed the magazine. "What are you reading?" she asked.

"The new *O Magazine*. Did you get your copy yet?"

"Yeah, I read it yesterday."

"What's up with that? You getting your copy before me? Oh . . . I think I forgot to check the mail yesterday. I probably have mine too. It's great. I'd love to get your thoughts on it.

Oprah says that she is delving into spirituality this month. Sounds right up our alley."

Avatari placed her drink on the coffee table, set her bag down by her feet, and sank heavily into the other comfy purple chair. "So . . . tell me what you're thinking."

"Well, I was reading what Oprah was saying, like Socrates, that the unexamined life is not worth living and that the unlived life isn't particularly worth examining.[22] I remember Dad telling me to examine my heart and see if I was in the faith." Lindsey paused for a moment. "He was pretty disappointed when I told him that I was moving beyond Christianity and considered myself to be more open-minded and tolerant of a variety of spiritual paths to the divine. I seriously didn't know what the big deal was. I wasn't rejecting Jesus. I just felt that Jesus, Buddha, and Lao Tzu, the author of *Tao Te Ching*, all pointed to the same unity of true consciousness that we all share in."

"One of the mistakes that human beings make is by believing that there is only one way to live, and we don't accept that there are diverse ways to being in the world."

Lindsey continued, "I know that Dad loved me. He would tell me, 'There is nothing that you could ever do to make me love you any less.' But I just don't know why he wasn't more open-minded about other faiths. He once tried to bring me back to Christianity by sending me a copy of Lee Strobel's *The Case for Christ*. Bless his heart, I never read the book. You know, going to MIT and all, he was brilliant and a great entrepreneur, but as far as his spirituality was concerned, sometimes I felt like he didn't have a clue about anything else except for his Bible-Belt, east Texas faith."

As she remembered these interactions with her dad, Lindsey found her eyes clouding with tears. She missed him so much, even those religious arguments that seemed so stressful at the time. Suddenly she remembered her father's warning about Oprah's "inclusive spirituality," and she gave a little laugh to fight back the tears. Avatari looked at her with concern, then reached over and gave Lindsey a side hug.

Lindsey's mind flashed back to the "Oprah" episode that her dad saw her watching with her mom.

She could remember the scene as though it were yesterday. She could almost smell the scent of her father's cologne as he joined them in the family room in front of the TV. On the show, Oprah was sitting down, saying, "One of the mistakes that human beings make is by believing that there is only one way to live, and we don't accept that there are diverse ways to being in the world."[23] She added, "There are many paths to what you call God. Her path may be something else, and when she gets there she may call it the Light."[24] An audience member, a middle-aged woman, stood up and disagreed with Oprah. She said that Jesus was the only way to heaven. Oprah responded in a terse voice, "There can't possibly be one way. I can't get into a religious argument with you right now."[25]

At that moment Lindsey's father had grunted, "That's nonsense! How about the fact that the Bible says, 'Salvation is found in no one else, for there is no other name under heaven given to men by which we must be saved.'[26] Jesus is the way, and the truth, and the life. No one comes to the Father except through him."[27]

Lindsey's mother looked lovingly at her husband as she kissed him on the cheek and said, "Honey, I agree with you, but Oprah is such a wonderful woman. She's just trying to make people feel good about themselves."

CHAPTER 4

Oprah's Tolerance

*Should we be open to other
spiritual paths?*

W hat are you thinking about?" Avatari interjected, snapping Lindsey back to attention.

"I was just remembering a time when I was at home over the holidays and I was watching 'Oprah' with Mom. At the time, I wasn't even an Oprah fan, but Mom totally was, like she still is now. I remember Dad telling Mom that he disagreed with Oprah's spiritual beliefs."

Lindsey hesitated for a second. "Avatari, what do you think?" she asked. "You're a Christian. Even though I don't always agree with your new way of thinking—which seems sort of like my old way of thinking—I still feel like you know so much more than I do. Do you really believe that there is only *one way* to salvation?"

Avatari smiled. "Yes, I do believe that salvation is through faith in Jesus only. I realize that it's not popular in our culture for a person to say that their religious beliefs are the only *true* religious beliefs. I used to get angry at Christians who said that *their* way was the right way."

"Really? You got mad? You seem like the type who never gets angry."

"You've obviously forgotten that time we lost our doubles tennis match," Avatari retorted with a smile.

"That's true," Lindsey laughed.

Avatari continued, "I used to get angry at Christians who said that *their* way was the only true way. While traveling the world, I used to think that each faith had one small but important part to contribute to the whole of religious truth. That's what I believed for most of my life, even after I stopped practicing Hinduism. Remember last year, when we read *Eat, Pray, Love?*"

"Remember what Elizabeth Gilbert wrote about people following different paths, depending on which one they consider best or most appropriate? She says that all paths eventually reach the same destination, just as rivers lead to the ocean."

"That was one of my favorite books that Oprah recommended."

"Remember what Elizabeth Gilbert wrote about people following different paths, depending on which one they consider best or most appropriate? She says that all paths eventually reach the same destination, just as rivers lead to the ocean. During my undergrad studies at Yale, even though I wasn't practicing Hinduism like my parents wanted me to, I believed that we all held part of the one truth. Like Oprah, I thought there couldn't possibly be just one way. I thought religious pluralism was a positive belief system."

"That's what I think right now," Lindsey interrupted. "What did you call it again?"

"Pluralism."

"So what's wrong with pluralism? Explain that for me, Aristotle!"

Avatari laughed. "Pluralism has several different meanings, but spiritually, *religious pluralism* teaches that multiple religions, often contradicting religions, are equally true. This is the dominant worldview of so many people in our culture—not just in India. The belief in religious or spiritual pluralism is dominant even right here in Austin. This type of religious pluralism is radically different from the pluralism that the United States was founded on, which tolerated and acknowledged that people—regardless of their religion—had the rights of citizenship. The new pluralism teaches that you don't just tolerate the multiplicity of religions, but now you must accept or look at them as equally true or valid."

"So is this the 'new awakening' that Eckhart Tolle and Oprah are talking about?" asked Lindsey.

"Not really. Pluralism has been around for ages. A philosopher named Celsus wrote a couple thousand years ago, 'It makes no difference if one invokes the highest God or Zeus or Adonai or Sabaoth or Amoun, as the Egyptians do, or Papaios, as the Scythians do.'"[28]

"Well, it seems new to me. My parents didn't believe spiritual pluralism in their Baptist church, and neither did the minister of the nondenominational church that I visited a couple weeks ago. They were so exclusive! Every pastor seems to believe that his or her way is the only right way."

"Well, *exclusivism* isn't a popular word today," commented Avatari as she sipped her latte.

"Tell me about it," Lindsey replied.

"It's unpopular because it teaches that one religion or spiritual belief is true, and anything that opposes it is false. In our society, we face opposition when we claim that our religion is absolutely true. In one of my undergraduate courses, I remember the professor and students laughing at this one guy because he said he believed that Jesus was the only way for salvation. Since I made the decision to follow Jesus, a couple of my friends in the philosophy department started mocking me. Did you happen to see that article in the new *O Magazine* by Martha Sherrill?"

"Yes! I just read it before you got here."

"This issue actually gives multiple examples of religious or spiritual pluralism," Avatari said.

Lindsey flipped the pages back to find the article she had been reading. She started quickly skimming the article and paused at some of the words from Sherrill:

> We're browsing the spiritual marketplace, dropping new ideas and philosophies into our carts—a smidgen of Buddhism, some New Testament, maybe a little tai chi tossed in.[29]

"Yeah, this describes what you're talking about. But look, Avatari—I don't get it. You're so loving and accepting of people no matter what their background is. Why did you reject the open-mindedness of pluralism?"

"Before I answer your question, let me share something I learned from philosopher Paul Copan when I first became a Christian. When I assert that Christian revelation is true, I'm not saying that all non-Christian religions or forms of spirituality are completely false in their teachings. I don't want to give you the impression that Oprah *never* says anything true about God. You should know I agree with a lot of what she stands for. I appreciate the kindness she has for people and all she does for the poor, and I think her shows are fun and encouraging. But as a Christ follower, I do believe that God's revelation is true and that other spiritual systems are false when they *contradict* the Bible."[30]

"Hmmm."

"Now, you asked me why I rejected the open-mindedness of pluralism?"

"Yes."

"Religious pluralism claims to be open-minded, but is it really? When we stop and think about the claims of religious or spiritual pluralism, we discover that actually, they don't accept any faith expression that is *not* pluralistic. Even though pluralism is touted at many universities as 'open-mindedness,' it's actually just another form of religious exclusivity."

"How?"

"Religious pluralism is really exclusive because it excludes anybody who doesn't believe it. Therefore, pluralism *excludes* the beliefs of hundreds of millions of Christians who claim that Jesus Christ is the *only way* for salvation." *Amen*

"Avatari, you know that we have never liked the word 'religion.' Oprah doesn't really use it. Eckhart Tolle doesn't like it. Most Christians don't use it anymore. Most of us prefer the word 'spirituality.' The book that we're reading for Rachel's book club on Wednesday says that most religions became divisive— that they were merely belief systems that people could identify to enhance their false sense of self."

Avatari nodded. "There is a lot of truth to that. Religions have definitely been manipulative throughout history. In fact, Jesus would often get ticked off at the religious leaders of the day because of the burdensome demands they would put on the ordinary people. Jesus has been saddened by many of the things done in his name. But to reject the word 'religion' because it entails a *belief system* and replace it with the word 'spirituality' could be self-defeating."

"How so?" Lindsey reached down, unzipped her Juicy Couture purse, and grabbed her copy of *A New Earth* by Eckhart Tolle. After trying to find what she was looking for, she read some words she previously highlighted in pink: "Many people are already aware of the difference between spirituality and religion. They realize that having a belief system—a set of thoughts that you regard as the absolute truth—does not make you spiritual no matter what the nature of those beliefs is."[31]

"Does Eckhart *believe* that?" asked Avatari.

"Yes!"

"Then that form of spirituality does have some set of *beliefs*. However, Jesus would have agreed with Eckhart that a set of belief systems does not make one spiritual. This is why Jesus called the Pharisees hypocrites. They did not practice what they believed. However, I read a comment made by a Christian author about Eckhart that it also does not make people spiritual if they present their belief system to others while claiming that their belief system is *not* a belief system, and that their beliefs are *not* beliefs."[32]

"Okay, I kind of see your point. But why are religious beliefs important?" Lindsey asked.

"For salvation, Jesus said that God requires us to *believe* in the one whom he sent. And just because the word 'religion' has been misused and gotten a bad rap among people of all spiritual beliefs does not necessarily mean that we need to lose it altogether. Religion can be very good, depending on how it is defined. The New Testament says, 'Religion that God our Father accepts as pure and faultless is this: to look after orphans and widows in their distress and to keep oneself from being polluted by the world.'[33] We are not saved by this religion, but who can argue with taking care of orphans and widows?"

"That's true. I believe that," Lindsey said with a smile, knowing that she had just used the word "believe." "Eastern religions like Hinduism and Buddhism are very open-minded. But Christianity really irks me because it's the only religion that says salvation occurs only one way—through Jesus."

Avatari responded, "Interestingly, it's not just Christianity that claims to be exclusively true. For example, Mohammed, the founder of Islam, claimed that Islam is the true religion."

"Well, it's obvious that Christianity and Islam are going to claim to be exclusively true, but what about others?"

"The teachers of Hinduism also said that *it* was the true religion. Then some Hindus decided to reject certain teachings of Hinduism, so they split off and started a new religion called Buddhism. Buddhism today includes hundreds of sects, each of which has its own set of religious beliefs. Religious pluralism rejects any of these religions that claim that their way is the *one way* that is true and correct. When you think about how many billions of people in the world follow these religions, you realize that most people are *not* religious or spiritual pluralists."

"Well, what about Oprah and some of her spiritual teachers? They seem open-minded to all beliefs."

"Lindsey, are they open-minded to Christianity?"

"Yes, I think so. Oprah's a Christian, and so are some of her guests."

"Do you think that Oprah is open to believing that salvation is *only* through Jesus and *not* through some other spiritual method, such as the awakening of consciousness that Eckhart Tolle writes about all faiths experiencing?"

"No. She says that she *doesn't* believe that, because that would be narrow-minded and put all the emphasis on one interpretation of Jesus."

"So are you telling me that Oprah—in her pluralism—is going to *exclude* the belief that says salvation for *all* people is *only* through Jesus?"

"Of course! That's just common sense."

"Why isn't she *open-minded* about the idea that salvation for all people could be through Christ alone?" Avatari paused for a second to let the words "open-minded" sink in. "Couldn't that be at least a little *narrow-minded* because she is *not* open-minded to the belief that salvation for all people is through Jesus?"

"How so?"

"Isn't she being exclusive to some extent when she *excludes* the belief that salvation for all people is only through Jesus?"

"I get your point. Even though religious or spiritual pluralism is touted as open-mindedness through the spiritual teachers that Oprah endorses, in one sense pluralism is just as exclusive as exclusivism, because it *excludes* any belief that doesn't agree with it."

"Precisely."

"Well, what about the famous parable of the blind men before the king of Benares, India, who touched different parts of the elephant? Since none of them can see, each gives a different description of what he believes the elephant to be—a rope, a tree, a large wall, a snake. Each of them argues that he has discovered the true nature of the elephant and that the others are wrong, when in reality all of them are partially right."[34]

"The true belief that the object is an elephant will exclude *the false beliefs that the object is a rope, a tree, a large wall, or a snake. Others may be sincere, but their sincerity will not change the fact that the object is an elephant!"*

"What are they touching?" Avatari asked.

"The elephant."

"Exactly. All of the blind men are wrong in what they claim the elephant to be. But the one telling the story understands what the truth is. The person who tells the story knows that the real object is *not* a rope, a tree, a large wall, or a snake. Those beliefs are false. The truth is that the real object is an elephant. The true belief that the object is an elephant will *exclude* the false beliefs that the object is a rope, a tree, a large wall, or a snake. The others may be sincere in their belief, but their sincerity will not change the fact that the object is an elephant!"

"Okay, Avatari. Maybe I shouldn't have tried to bring that illustration up with you." Lindsey glanced at her watch. "Girl, I know you have to go to teach Pilates, and we're both tired from being up all hours of the night. Let's talk about this more at book club on Wednesday. My brain needs a break."

"Okay, let's continue this conversation on Wednesday."

"Definitely..." She paused. "Maybe Oprah's pluralism actually reveals her closed-mindedness in some areas," Lindsey said. "But couldn't this whole thing about Jesus be true for you but not true for me?"

"We're probably going to talk about the nature of truth at Rachel's because Eckhart brings it up in *A New Earth*," said Avatari. "Shall we wait and talk about this on Wednesday?"

"Sure," responded Lindsey.

"I'll see you then!" said Avatari. She grabbed her purse and the two girls walked together toward the glass exit doors.

CHAPTER 5

The Book Club with Eckhart Tolle

Is truth absolute or relative?

For over two years, Lindsey, Avatari, Maria, Rachel, and Beth had managed to meet fairly regularly for their Wednesday night book club at Rachel's house. Rachel, a stay-at-home mom in her late thirties, constantly commended Avatari and Lindsey for staying faithful to the group during grad school. "Ladies," she would tell them, "if you ever need to skip our book discussion to study, I completely understand."

On occasion, either Lindsey or Avatari had skipped the book club to finish a paper or study for an upcoming test, but for the most part both girls found it to be a pleasurable, peaceful place of community in times of stress. Throughout the year, many other graduate students from UT were invited, but most of them, owing to the time constraints imposed on them by their studies, were not as committed. Rachel, who had earned a master's of divinity degree from Southern Methodist University ten years earlier, was completely empathetic.

Over the past two years, many of the books that Rachel and the girls picked to read had been featured in Oprah's book club. Others included books by other guests on Oprah's shows. The books included *The Secret* by Rhonda Byrne, *The Power of Now* by Eckhart Tolle, *Eat, Pray, Love* by Elizabeth Gilbert, *A Return to Love* by Marianne Williamson, *Discover the Power Within You* by Eric Butterworth, *Quantum Wellness* by Kathy Freston, and *Change Your Thoughts—Change Your Life* by Dr. Wayne W. Dyer.

Recently, the group had been reading and discussing Eckhart Tolle's *A New Earth*. After complimenting the delicious red wine that Beth had brought back from her recent honeymoon in Italy, Rachel said, "Let's go ahead and get started with *A New Earth*."

Maria laughed, but then her face got serious. "Well, if you can turn this red wine back into water and feed five thousand people with this plate of brownies, then I might believe you are the Truth."

Looking at Rachel, Maria, and Avatari, Beth said, "I know you philosophers and religious scholars probably find Eckhart Tolle easy to understand, but I have to admit that I find it a little challenging. It's somewhat enlightening, but we fashion designers don't normally talk about the nature of truth. What's the big debate?"

Rachel chimed in, "Avatari's the philosopher, not me! But we do need to talk about whether truth is absolute or relative. It can be dangerous when a person claims that their belief or doctrine about God is absolute truth and anything opposed to it is false! I believe that truth does exist, but one person's perspective of truth can be different from another's and that truth changes frequently." Lindsey smiled at Avatari, remembering their discussion at Starbucks.

Rachel continued, "Well, let's look at what Eckhart has to say." Turning to the section "Truth: Relative or Absolute," Rachel read, "All religions are equally false and equally true, depending on how you use them."[35]

"What do you think about that, girls?" she asked.

Lindsey commented, "I tend to agree that truth can be relative or absolute. And truth isn't just what Jesus said or some other statement about God; truth is inseparable from who we are. Our being, our very nature, is really the only Truth, with a capital *T*. Therefore, I can say, 'I am the Absolute Truth.'"

Maria, a conservative Christian who had taken some courses at a theological seminary, interrupted, "But isn't that kind of arrogant for you to claim, as a limited human being, that you are 'the Absolute Truth'? I think Jesus is the only person who can make that claim." She reached over to grab one of the brownies that Rachel had laid out on the coffee table. As she settled back in her chair, Maria felt the familiar strain on the waistband of her jeans and said, "I should definitely not be eating this. I'm starting my diet tomorrow."

"Ooh, I've got to have one of those, too!" Lindsey said as she grabbed a brownie and responded to Maria's comments. "Oprah says that Christ came to show us that we can discover our own 'Christ-consciousness.'[36] Eckhart says that according to the Bible we can become the Truth, with a capital *T*, as Jesus became the Truth.[37] I grew up in a church in the Bible Belt. I used to believe—like you do—that Jesus was greater than us, but now I tend to agree more with Oprah and Eckhart. Maybe Jesus was no more God than you and I are. Maybe we're all just part of the Ultimate Being that we call God or Universal Energy or that Eckhart calls Consciousness. Eckhart doesn't feel that it is arrogant for me to say, 'I am the Way, the Truth, and the Life.' If Jesus said it, why can't I?"

Maria laughed, but then her face got serious. "Well, if you can turn this red wine back into water and feed five thousand people with this plate of brownies, then I might believe you are the Truth."

"Maria," Lindsey responded, "I know that you're thinking about it from a conservative standpoint. It sounds like you agree with my old pastor. Incidentally, he would disagree with your drinking that wine. Just open your mind for a sec. Listen to what Tolle says: 'The Truth is inseparable from who you are. Yes, you *are* the Truth. If you look for it elsewhere, you will be deceived every time.'"[38]

Up until this point in the discussion Avatari had remained silent and peaceful in the midst of the debate. But now she jumped in with a question.

"What if the 'elsewhere' that someone looked to was Jesus? Does that mean they're deceived?"

"I don't think that counts," commented Lindsey.

"Why doesn't it count? It's ironic that Eckhart quotes Jesus to make his point about the foolishness for looking outside ourselves for the Truth." Avatari continued, "Because a few words later in John 14:6, Jesus adds, 'No one comes to Father except through *me*.' The emphasis is on experiencing a relationship with his Father through *him* and knowing *him*, not ourselves."

Trying to keep things light, Lindsey replied, "Let me ask you, what do you all think Oprah believes? Does she believe that truth is absolute or relative?"

Rachel commented, "She probably agrees with whatever Eckhart says. A couple days ago, I read in *O Magazine* where Oprah said Eckhart Tolle is 'a prophet of our time.'"[39]

"Rachel, do you have the most recent copy of *O Magazine*?" asked Maria.

"Yes, it's right over here," Rachel responded as she grabbed it from the side table next to Avatari.

While flipping through to find the article she was looking for, Maria continued, "That's pretty strong language—to describe him as a prophet of our time and not just as a 'good spiritual teacher.' Oprah tends to follow Eckhart when he says that all truths are relative except for the absolute truth—that he, along with us, are the Truth with a capital *T*. In other words, we are part of God. Yet Oprah also seems to promote authors who just believe that truth is relative."

"Aha. Here is what I wanted to read to you. In this same issue of *O Magazine*, Kelly Corrigan wrote an article called 'The Doubters Dilemma.' Listen to this, girls. Corrigan writes: 'Only two years ago, children were still being taught to believe that poor Pluto was a planet. If history teaches us anything, it's that the truth is subject to change.'"[40]

Beth commented, "Why does it matter? Why are all of you getting so fired up about truth?"

Lindsey responded, "I think that those who believe in absolute truth with regard to their beliefs about God are the ones who make such a big deal about it. Let me see that magazine for a second. I want to show you a quote I read on Oprah's section on spirituality. Hold on a second...let me find it. This is by Martha Beck. Listen to this, 'In short, absolutism is the opiate that turns the masses into ideology-addicted murderers, whether religious or irreligious.'"[41]

"Is that absolutely true?" asked Avatari.

"Is what absolutely true?" asked Lindsey.

Avatari spoke in her typically calm tone of voice, but her confidence shone through as she said, "Her statement that absolutism is the opiate that turns the masses into ideology-addicted murderers, whether religious or irreligious. If her statement is simply *relatively* true, then it may not be true for anyone else, so why should any of us consider it a valid opinion? If that statement is *absolutely* true, she has embraced that ideology herself."

Beth interrupted, "Hold up. You're getting over my head. You never did answer my question, Avatari. Why does this whole 'truth' thing even matter?"

Avatari responded, "In every area of our lives, we demand truth. We insist on knowing the truth in our daily lives. We have expectations that the court will convict only the truly guilty. We expect to know the truth in our relationships. Most people don't enter a relationship expecting their loved one to be untruthful or unfaithful. This is true even with simple daily tasks: We expect the banker to tell us the truth about our finances. We want the doctor to tell us the truth about our medical condition. When you need to use a public restroom, you expect the truth when you read the 'male' or 'female' sign. Now, if God is the greatest Being there is, and in him we discover the purpose of life, our salvation, and our destiny, shouldn't we want to discover the truth about him?

"Let me give an analogy to illustrate why I believe truth is important," she continued. "Let's suppose hypothetically that someone discovered the cure to cancer—the cure not just to some cancers but all cancer. Now, the most loving thing for the individual who discovered that truth to do is to share that truth with those who are in need of a cure. If God is the greatest Being there is, and someone has discovered a truth about him that will not only influence our physical health but our spiritual health as well, wouldn't it be loving to share that knowledge with others?"

"I suppose," commented Beth. "But how do you *know* if something is true? What *is* truth?"

Maria jumped in, "That's what Pilate asked Jesus. The Bible says that Jesus is the embodiment of Absolute Truth."

Lindsey responded, "But can't we become Truth with a capital *T*, like Eckhart says?"

"Have you ever told a lie, Linds?" asked Avatari.

"Of course," Lindsey admitted.

Avatari continued, "Then how could you claim to be the Absolute Truth with a capital *T*? Jesus is the only Person who is Truth with a capital *T* in his very essence. We, on the other hand, change our minds and make mistakes, but only God is the embodiment of absolute truth. However, Jesus has called us to *know* the truth. Jesus said, 'You will know the truth and the truth will set you free.'[42] Having a knowledge of truth is very important."

"So how do you define truth?" asked Beth.

Avatari continued, "Many definitions of truth fail, but a good definition of truth is 'that which corresponds to reality.' Simply put, truth is 'telling it like it is.'"

"But like Maria read from the magazine about the planet Pluto, truth is subject to change," commented Rachel.

Avatari continued, "People's *opinions*, *theories*, *beliefs*, and *feelings* about the truth may change, but the actual truth is unchanging and absolute. Let me add that even though there may be disagreement, the truth about reality is knowable. You and I can have a knowledge of the truth even though our knowledge may not be exhaustive."

Avatari continued, "So . . . did the truth about Pluto change?"

She let the girls ponder that for a second. "The truth about Pluto didn't change. People's opinions or beliefs changed but the *truth* about Pluto was true and unchanging, even if people disagreed about it. Do you mind if I go out to my car and find that book by Paul Copan? There's a quote I wanted to read to you."

"Sure," said Lindsey.

Rachel took the opportunity to ask the girls if she could refill their glasses, and when Avatari returned with not only the Copan book but a whole stack of books, the girls were back in their places.

"Nerd!" Lindsey jokingly commented to Avatari with a smile.

"Yeah, she's a hot nerd that every single guy at my wedding was checking out," commented Beth.

Sensing that the girls were about to take a major detour, Avatari stepped in quickly and said, "Okay, listen to this quote about absolute truth:

Although some states have given up trying to figure out whom to blame for car accidents—hence 'no-fault' insurance—truth matters. And when the stakes are raised—when a child crossing the street is struck and killed, for example—finding the truth becomes essential. Serious circumstances remind us that the difficulty of finding truth is no excuse for not looking."[43]

Rachel commented, "But Avatari, can't some truths be absolute and other truths be relative?"

"Great question." Avatari turned to another book she had pulled out of her car called *I Don't Have Enough Faith to Be an Atheist* by Norman Geisler and Frank Turek. "Okay, here are some truths about truth:

- Truth is discovered, not invented. It exists independent of anyone's knowledge of it. (Gravity existed prior to Newton.)

- Truth is transcultural; if something is true, it is true for all people, in all places, at all times (2+2=4 for everyone, everywhere, at every time).

- Truth is unchanging even though our *beliefs* about truth change.

- Beliefs cannot change a fact, no matter how sincerely they are held. (Someone can sincerely believe that the world is flat, but that only makes that person sincerely mistaken.)

- Truth is not affected by the attitude of the one professing it. (An arrogant person does not make the truth he professes false. A humble person does not make the error he professes true.)"[44]

"Wow, that's really interesting. This absolute truth stuff is starting to make some sense to me," Beth commented.

Avatari smiled and continued, "Today, some people are attempting to deny absolute truth and the simple laws of logic.

When this happens, a person often commits the fallacy of giving a *self-defeating statement*."

"Okay, Miss Know-It-All," said Lindsey, "explain that for all of us non-philosophers."

Avatari continued, "A *self-defeating statement* is a statement that fails to meet its own standard. For example, if someone said, 'I can't speak a word of English' in English, that would be a self-defeating statement. Why? Because she just spoke that sentence *in English!* In the same way, if someone says, 'There is no absolute truth!' you could respond by saying, 'Is that absolutely true?' If so, the person has just contradicted herself. If someone says, 'You can't know any truth about God!' you could respond by saying, 'How do you *know* that God is unknowable?' That in itself is a truth that the person is claiming to know. It's a self-defeating statement."

"But Avatari, you are just using Western logic, which is the *either-or* logic," responded Rachel. "Oprah, Eckhart, and most open-minded spiritual people in the East use *both-and* logic. Isn't that more fair?"

Maria jumped in, "What's up with a blond-haired, blue-eyed Texas girl telling a girl born in India that she doesn't understand Eastern logic!"

Rachel continued. "Point taken. But while I was in grad school, I became open-minded to the Eastern logic that Eckhart holds to. Avatari, Western logic is too narrow-minded because it holds to absolute truth. Followers of Eastern logic hold to *both-and*. So salvation is not *either* through Jesus *or* nothing else, but both through Jesus *and* other ways."

Avatari commented, "Have you thought that through carefully?"

"I absolutely believe that," commented Rachel. "There certainly are two types of logic: one Western and one Eastern. I prefer Eastern logic, which is *both-and*."

Avatari leaned forward. "Rachel, are you telling me that I must *either* embrace both-and logic *or* remain closed-minded?"

Rachel sheepishly admitted, "The *either-or* does seem to pop up, doesn't it?"[45]

Lindsey smiled at Avatari's witty question. "That really makes sense, Avatari. But what about Eckhart? What does he believe about logic and truth?"

"Every time Eckhart tries to deny logic, he ends up using it. Over and over throughout *A New Earth*, he ends up affirming what he denies. For example, Eckhart speaks against churches, sects, cults, or religious movements that are closed to any alternative interpretations of reality. But it seems to me that Eckhart is closed to an interpretation of reality that is an alternative to *his* interpretation of reality."[46]

"How so?" asked Lindsey.

"We could pick some obvious examples. Obviously, he would be opposed to the alternative interpretation of reality offered by a radical Islamic terrorist who says we should start wars in the name of God. I am very thankful that he is opposed to this false interpretation of reality, but I think Eckhart should admit that he is indeed closed to certain alternative interpretations of reality. Eckhart would also be closed to the alternative interpretation of reality by Bible study teacher Beth Moore or evangelist Billy Graham or pastor Rick Warren that says salvation is only through Jesus.

"As is quite clear in his books, he wants us to believe *his* interpretation of reality where we need to awaken the consciousness within and Jesus Christ is not the only way, and he wants us to let go of anything that opposes his view."

"What's another example of Eckhart affirming what he denies?" asked Rachel.

Avatari was quick to respond. "Oh, I highlighted this one. Let's see here. On page twenty-five, Eckhart writes, 'Everything, a bird, a tree, even a simple stone, and certainly a human being, is ultimately *unknowable.*'[47] He says that all these things are unknowable, but how does he *know* that? I feel like I'm doing all of the talking. Would somebody else please read starting on page twenty-five?" asked Avatari. "Eckhart is going to speak against the use of words by using words!"

Lindsey volunteered, "I'll read. 'Words, no matter whether they are vocalized and made into sounds or remain unspoken as thoughts, can cast an almost hypnotic spell upon you.'"[48] Lindsey paused and asked, "Well, I agree with that to some extent, but if it is the case that words can almost cast a hypnotic spell upon you, then why is he writing a 316-page book filled with thousands and thousands of words? Is he trying to cast a spell on us?"

"If it is the case that words can almost cast a hypnotic spell upon you, then why is he writing a 316-page book filled with thousands and thousands of words? Is he trying to cast a spell on us?"

"I have to be honest, I have never thought about it quite like this before," commented Rachel. "Why does Oprah say that Eckhart is 'a brilliant, authentic voice who never fails to inspire me more'?"

Avatari paused a moment and commented, "I'm not exactly sure."

As she reached for her third brownie of the evening, Maria commented, "I think he's an overrated idiot. He really hasn't come up with anything new. We ought to start on a new book."

"I don't agree with everything that Eckhart says, but I wouldn't call him an idiot," Avatari softly reprimanded. "As a Cambridge graduate, he is intelligent and does say some things that are true. But he definitely says things that contradict the simple laws of logic or even his own teachings, like I just pointed out. So, rather than calling him an idiot, we should simply reveal his inaccurate statements that contradict the truth and even what he teaches."

"I'm sorry. I shouldn't have said that," commented Maria, "I'll take responsibility for my unkind comment about Eckhart as a person, but I won't just blame my ego for my sin like he would!" she added to lessen her embarrassment.

"What do you mean by blaming your ego?" asked Rachel.

Maria continued, "Remember? Tolle teaches that since everyone is ultimately God or 'consciousness,' our ego, which really is an illusion, is responsible for all of our sins. But contrary to Tolle, I'll take responsibility for my own sins. I still get frustrated with the millions of people who buy into this phony spirituality, saying it's 'all new' and claiming to be so tolerant. Yet they're extremely intolerant toward the interpretation of the Bible that says salvation is though Christ alone. I just don't understand why so many Christians are drawn to this hypocritical so-called tolerance. Didn't Paul the apostle warn that this would happen? I think it was in the last letter that he wrote before he was martyred for saying salvation was only through Jesus. Do you know what I am talking about, Avatari?"

Avatari commented, "Are you referring to Paul's last words to Timothy—something about staying true to sound doctrine even though in the future many false spiritual teachers will try to say that doctrine is not important and will believe what they want to believe?"

"Yes, that's exactly what I'm talking about," said Maria.

Rachel said, "I've got a Bible right here. Second Timothy, last chapter, right? Who wants to read this?"

"I will," volunteered Beth.

"Before God and Christ Jesus, who is going to judge the living and the dead, and by His appearing and His Kingdom, I solemnly charge you: proclaim the message; persist in it whether convenient or not; rebuke, correct, and encourage with great patience and teaching. For the time will come when they will not tolerate sound doctrine, but according to their own desires, will accumulate teachers for themselves because they have an itch to hear something new. They will turn away from hearing the truth and will turn aside to myths."[49]

Rachel interrupted. "Hold on. Just because Oprah and Eckhart don't seem very positive toward doctrine and are talking about a 'something new,' can we be certain that this verse that was written two thousand years ago is referring to teachers like them? That seems a little farfetched."

"Okay, maybe it's not specifically toward them, but I think it is talking about false teachers like them," commented Maria. "Let me ask you something, Rachel. Oprah, Eckhart, and many of these spiritual teachers say they are against doctrine. Over and over, these 'New Thought' teachers say they don't believe in doctrine. How do they define doctrine?"

"Well, doctrine of course is a set of beliefs that a church or institution says that we ought to believe in," responded Rachel.

Maria quickly responded, "Well, Oprah and Eckhart certainly have doctrine too. Their doctrine says that you ought not have beliefs or doctrine. Their doctrine says that you *should not* say Jesus is the only way. Their doctrine teaches that you are the Way, the Truth, and the Life. Their doctrine says that we are part of the one universal force that some refer to as God. Their doctrine says that you can call this Being whatever you like. Their doctrine says you *ought not* say someone's sexual behavior is wrong. It seems like they say they are against doctrine only so they can come up with their own doctrine..."

"Okay, I get your point," Rachel interrupted. "I still disagree with you, but maybe they do have some beliefs. Even if they have doctrine, I like theirs much better than some of those antiquated doctrines from Paul in the New Testament. From your point of view, you think that Eckhart Tolle is a false spiritual teacher, but the truth is that Oprah recommends many other wonderful spiritual teachers as well. Remember Rhonda Byrne's *The Secret?* The teachings of *The Secret* have been around since before the time of Jesus."

CHAPTER 6

Rhonda Byrne's
The Secret

Does The Secret *work?*

W hen Rachel mentioned Rhonda Byrne's *The Secret*, Lindsey's mind traveled back in time to a scene that occurred at Plano Presbyterian Hospital four months earlier.

Four months ago
Presbyterian Hospital, Plano, Texas
"Honey," said Lindsey's mom, Barbara. "We're just going to keep on believing that your father is going to recover." Lindsey and her mother sat beside her father, who was resting. "We just have to trust that this cancer is an illusion and that your father is going to come out of it. Your father never let negative thoughts come into his mind, and we must have faith that he's going to come out better than before. He has a lot of faith in God. Let's just claim God's promises and believe in the law of attraction. The law of attraction says that we attract whatever we think."

"Mom, you're not helping!" Lindsey lashed out in impatience at her mother. She was tired of hearing her talk about being positive, she was tired of being at the hospital day after day, and mostly she was just sad and tired. She had been nothing but patient and supportive of her mother up to this point, but she found herself at the end of her patience. "You're not being realistic about this whole faith thing. Your name-and-claim-it, 'law of attraction' attitude is getting on my nerves. Even if God is with us right now, I don't think he is a finite being that we can manipulate with our thoughts."

"Lindsey, sweetheart, don't say those negative words. You have to *believe*. Remember that book *The Secret* that your father gave me for my birthday?"

Lindsey had already read the book in Rachel's book club, and she had really liked it. She once told the book club that it helped her succeed in law school. But she didn't feel like discussing it at the moment. "Yeah, I remember the book, but the doctors were clear. They just told us that the cancer isn't going away."

"Well, it will if we *believe* it will. *The Secret* may just inspire him to get better. He told me a few weeks ago that *The Secret* was one of the best books he ever read. It reminded him of many of the inspirational teachers like John Canfield and Wayne Dyer from his sales training conventions."

Barbara looked at her daughter. "Lindsey, your father is such a positive thinker! If we want him to get healthy, we need to visualize health for him. The law of attraction is powerful. I read about one woman who was diagnosed with breast cancer and was cured in three months without chemotherapy or radiation. She did so by visualizing herself as well and watching funny movies on television.[50] I believe that your father is lying there generating positive thoughts in his dreams right now and I'm certainly not going to work against him by thinking negatively. In fact, I'm going to start reading *The Secret* to your father when he wakes up to be sure he doesn't forget."

Suddenly, Lindsey's father stirred in his hospital bed and opened his eyes.

"Honey, are you waking up?" asked Barbara.

"Yes, beautiful, I'm awake," he said.

"Good! I was just telling Lindsey that I wanted to read you some inspirational thoughts."

"Okay. Might as well, since I'm not going anywhere. Thank you, love."

Barbara pulled the book out of her purse and began reading portions from the chapter entitled "The Secret to Health":

> When people are completely focused on what's wrong and their symptoms, they will perpetuate it. The healing will not occur until they shift their attention from being sick to being well. Because that's the law of attraction.[51]

> Think thoughts of perfection. Illness cannot exist in a body that has harmonious thoughts. Know there is only perfection, and as you observe perfection you must summon that to you. Imperfect thoughts are the cause of all humanity's ills, including disease, poverty, and unhappiness. When we think negative thoughts we are cutting ourselves off from our rightful heritage. Declare and intend, "I think perfect thoughts. I see only perfection. I am perfection."[52]

> You can *think* your way to the perfect state of health, the perfect body, the perfect weight, and eternal youth. You can bring it into being, through your consistent thinking of perfection.[53]

Lindsey's father calmly interrupted her mother. "Sweetie, I appreciate your reading to me, but right now I'd rather have you read the Bible to me. The Holy Spirit has put this on my heart. In these last couple of weeks, God has been teaching me the true secret—not the 'law of attraction,' but the secret of being content in whatever circumstances he's put me in. I'm all about positive thinking, and I believe God has the power to heal me today, but I also feel that we need to trust Jesus no matter what happens. God is not a genie in a bottle that just submits to a force of faith or words we speak. He is the sovereign ruler of the universe. The apostle Paul said, 'I consider that our present sufferings are not worth comparing with the glory that will be revealed in us.'[54] Can you please read me some Scripture? Read to me from where Paul was locked up in prison, and writing to the church at Philippi."

Barbara remembered reading about Paul's life in the book in Acts. Though he was an extremely optimistic person, his writings seemed contrary to *The Secret*. Even though he felt severe physical suffering, Paul experienced remarkable spiritual confidence and a deep inner joy. He knew that he was living out God's sovereign will for his life.

As Barbara read from the letter to the Philippians, a nurse appeared in the doorway. Barbara stopped reading as the nurse brought in a cheerful bouquet from Lindsey's friend Maria back in Austin.

"I just love that Maria!" he said. "She's so thoughtful."

"She is," agreed Lindsey. She sat with her legs hanging over the side of the green armchair in the corner of the hospital room and stared out the window, letting the verses of Philippians filter through her mind. Her mom read, "For it has been given to you on behalf of Christ not only to believe on Him, but *also to suffer for him*."[55]

Barbara continued reading. "I know what it is to be in need, and I know what it is to have plenty. I have learned *the secret* of being content in any and every situation, whether well fed or hungry, whether living in plenty or in want. I can do everything through him who gives me strength. Yet it was good of you to share in my troubles."[56]

As her mom read the words from the apostle Paul, she began to ponder the implications for her own spiritual journey. *Paul believed that sometimes pain and suffering can be used to draw us closer to God and help us understand the most important things in life*, Lindsey mused to herself. *Maybe he can make something good come from my dad's illness.*

The present
Wednesday night book club, Rachel's house

"Hello? Earth to Lindsey!" Rachel waved her hand in front of Lindsey's face.

"Oh, sorry," Lindsey said. "I guess I just zoned out for a second."

"Lindsey, what do you think about Rhonda Byrne's view of God? I mean, do you think that Rhonda Byrne is telling the truth about God's nature? Surely you wouldn't say that she's a false teacher, would you?"

Lindsey, in a lame attempt to pretend that she had been paying attention to the conversation, commented, "Tell me again what she says about who God is. It's been a while since I read *The Secret*."

> *"Well, basically, pantheism teaches that God is all. The universe is God. You and I are God . . . Pantheism is opposed to the Christian world-view of* theism, *which says that God* made *all."*

"Her beliefs seem very pantheistic to me," commented Avatari.

"Avatari, define pantheistic for me," said Lindsey.

"Well, basically, pantheism teaches that God *is* all. The universe is God. You and I are God. The earth, the ground, the flowers, and everything around is permeated by the divine Being. Hinduism, the primary pantheistic religion, teaches that the ultimate Being is Brahman. Pantheism is opposed to the Christian worldview of *theism*, which says that God *made* all. Christianity, Islam, and Judaism teach that God *made* the universe and that God *made* you and me. The Bible says that even though God is omnipresent, he is also transcendent (beyond us), and clearly distinct from us. Christianity says that God made us, but we are not God. Since truth is absolute, it is impossible for both of these worldviews to be true because they specifically contradict each other. However, *The Secret* says you are God in a physical body and that you are all-powerful. Rhonda Byrne says that we are One. We are all connected, and we are all part of the One Supreme Mind, or the One Consciousness, or the One Creative Source."[57]

While Avatari expounded philosophically on the nature of pantheism, Lindsey thought she heard a faint buzzing in her purse. She pulled out her cell phone and saw that she had missed a call from her aunt Susan and there was a text message: "Emergency with your mom. Call me ASAP!"

Lindsey gasped and jumped up. "Sorry—I have to make a phone call." She ran outside to call her aunt, but she just got voice mail. Terrifying scenarios flooded Lindsey's mind as she pressed redial. She couldn't help but think of what had happened on Thanksgiving...

Fifteen days ago
Plano, Texas

Without Dad, Thanksgiving back home just didn't seem normal to Lindsey at all. She looked over at her mom. The red wine sloshed over the brim of her mother's glass and splashed onto the front of her blue and white print blouse. It began to dribble slowly toward her lap, but Barbara seemed completely unaware, or unconcerned, or both.

"Mom, how much have you been drinking lately?" asked Lindsey with a furrow in her brow. "I don't think I've ever seen you like this."

Barbara swung her arm in what was supposed to be a carefree dismissal of a silly notion, but as more liquid sloshed out of the glass, she only confirmed her daughter's suspicions. "Sweetheart, it's okay. I've only had a teensy bit."

"Mom . . . you hardly ever used to drink, but now every time I'm over you have a glass of wine or a martini in your hand. I know it's been tough with Daddy gone, but you need to be careful. Why don't you call me more? I'm here for you."

Barbara's face crumpled as though she'd been holding her placid expression in place with a very thin thread and someone had just snipped it. "I'm just so sorry I kept pushing that law of attraction stuff on you. I really thought it was going to help Dad make it, but you were right. He's gone."

"Mom, it's okay. Whenever you need to talk, call me. Why don't you give me that glass and I'll make you a cup of tea?"

The present

"Lindsey? Lindsey. Are you there?" Again, jolted back to reality by the sound of her name, Lindsey felt a flood of relief pouring through her as she realized that her aunt had finally answered the phone. But a feeling of dread quickly followed in anticipation of the news she was about to receive.

"I'm here. What's wrong with Mom?"

"I found her unconscious a couple of hours ago . . ." She paused to choke back a sob. "Lindsey, she overdosed on painkillers. She has strong vitals but she's still unconscious."

"Oh, my God," Lindsey moaned. "Mom, no . . ." Her mind raced. *A suicide attempt? Mom, I can't lose you now. Not on top of everything that's happened.*

Lindsey didn't even remember hanging up the phone. She raced back into the house. "My mom's in the hospital! I have to go see her."

"What happened?" the girls gasped. Lindsey just couldn't force herself to tell them. Avatari took one look at the pained expression on Lindsey's face and said, "I'm coming with you. I'll drive."

CHAPTER 7

"Oprah and Friends" on XM Radio

Is God all? Or did God make all?

Lindsey jumped into the passenger seat of Avatari's navy blue Honda Element. She laid her head back against the headrest and sighed in anguish. *This can't be happening to me*, she thought.

After a few minutes, she said, "Avatari, I just can't believe my mom did this. It seems like she's lost her faith completely." She paused for a moment. "She's been drinking way too much lately. I mean, being a conservative Christian, she used to hardly ever drink when I was growing up, but she seems to have gotten off track after Dad's death. I was so depressed when I found out that Dad only had a couple weeks to live, but Mom was strong in her faith then, even leading up to his death. She told me to just keep believing and thinking positive thoughts about wellness." She paused.

"But that all changed a few months ago, when Dad died. All of his positive thinking, and all of hers, didn't work. She was really angry, I think. Rhonda Byrne's law of attraction in her book *The Secret* didn't work. All the stuff that her favorite 'word of faith' teachers on television said didn't work, either. She felt like they had deceived her. I guess Mom got into *The Secret* a little too much."

Lindsey was quiet for a minute, thinking about her mom. "I've really tried to comfort Mom and remind her that death is natural and happens to everyone. It was just Dad's time. At least he had faith in God and was at peace when he died. I tried to comfort her with the thought that he's in heaven, cancer-free and waiting for her."

"Do you believe that?" asked Avatari.

"Yeah, I guess I do. But it's hard for me to comfort someone spiritually when I'm not exactly sure what I believe anymore. I just have a lot of questions about who God is. I mean, are we all part of God, like some of Oprah's friends believe? Or is God different from us, like I used to believe when I was a little girl? I just hope that I know the right thing to say to Mom so I can give her some inspiration to keep pressing on. I just don't know what I'd do . . ." Her voice trailed off. She knew she'd break down if she said another word.

"Can I please say a little prayer for your mom right now, while I'm driving with my eyes on the road?" asked Avatari.

Lindsey nodded, full of emotion.

"Dear Heavenly Father, I come to you now and want to thank you for your unfailing love. I acknowledge that you are all-powerful and all-knowing. You understand what Lindsey is going through, and I thank you that you love her unconditionally. I pray for your protection for Barbara and thank you that she is alive. I pray that you would help her to recover quickly. Dear God, will you please comfort and encourage Barbara and Lindsey spiritually as well? They have been through so much lately and we don't really understand why. Help Barbara to know how valuable she is to you and that you have a purpose for her life. Thank you, Father, for the blessing that Barbara and Lindsey have been to me. Their friendship means so much. In Jesus' name. Amen."

"Thanks, Av. That was a sweet prayer," Lindsey said as she wiped her tears away with a tissue, smearing her mascara in the process.

Lindsey balled up the tissue, rested her head against the seat, and looked out the window for a while. After about twenty minutes, she asked Avatari, "Can I turn on the radio? I really need to be distracted right now."

"Sure, go ahead."

As Lindsey was flipping channels, she decided to stop at "Oprah and Friends" on XM Radio. The host, Marianne Williamson, with whom the girls were familiar, was teaching her seminar *A Course in Miracles*. She told her audience,

Marianne asked the audience to respond by saying: "My salvation comes from me. Nothing outside of me can hold me back. Within me is the world's salvation and my own."

"Spiritual transformation begins with shifting your physical perceptions of what's real. If you think what you see and hear is all that's real, you'll be dictated by the limits of your senses."[58] Then Williamson asked the audience to repeat: "This table does not mean anything. This chair does not mean anything. This hand does not mean anything."[59]

A few minutes later, Marianne asked the audience to repeat: "God is in this coat hanger. God is in this magazine. God is in this finger. God is in this lamp. God is in that body. God is in that door. God is in that waste basket."[60]

She asked the audience to respond by saying: "My salvation comes from me. Nothing outside of me can hold me back. Within me is the world's salvation and my own."[61]

After she heard that, Lindsey turned down the volume to ask Avatari some questions. "Avatari, I know earlier you were telling me about the nature of God. I really wasn't paying attention but I right now I think it's important for me to really know who God is. You mentioned something about pantheism, which says 'all is God,' and I don't really see the problem with it. I mean, especially in times like this you want to know that God is near. The God of Christianity seems kind of far away to me sometimes."

Avatari responded, "I understand. Sometimes we all feel like God is far off. There was a time when King David in the Bible cried out, 'My God, my God, why have you forsaken me?'[62] But even though we may feel forsaken, God is still with us. Let me explain it this way: God is both distinct from us and near to us. He is holy, which means 'set apart.' Yet God is also near. Christianity does teach us that God is omnipresent; that means he is present everywhere. He is near and yet unlimited by any particular location. In one my favorite pieces of literature in the Bible, David later recognized this truth saying to God:

> Where can I go from Your Spirit?
> Where can I flee from Your presence?
> If I go up to heavens, You are there;
> If I make my bed in the depths, You are there.
> If I rise on the wings of the dawn, if I settle on the far
> side of the sea,
> even there Your hand will guide me;
> Your right hand will hold me fast.[63]

"That is much more beautiful than his 'forsaken me' poetry," Lindsey commented.

Avatari continued. "I agree. But just because God is near doesn't mean that everything at its core is ultimately God. God is clearly distinct from you, me, or anything else—such as a magazine or chair. For me, as a former Hindu, understanding the distinction between pantheism and theism was one of my biggest obstacles."

"What made you change your mind?" asked Lindsey.

Avatari went on, "One contemporary Christian theologian who got my attention was Dr. Norman Geisler. He opened my mind to understand that absolute pantheism is self-defeating. The absolute pantheist claims, 'I am God.' But God is the changeless Absolute. However, Oprah and Eckhart Tolle teach that humanity goes through the process of change called awakening, which others may call enlightenment, because they have this awareness. So how could people be God when people change, but God does not change?[64] We change, but God never does. His characteristics, including his love for us, are constant and enduring. It's impossible for God to change, because he's a different kind of being than we are."

"I'm still struggling to understand the distinction," Lindsey said, "and it may just be because my mind is on my mom right now. My natural inclination is still the worldview of pantheism."

Avatari moved her right hand from the steering wheel and patted Lindsey's arm. "Are you sure you're up to talking about this now, Linds?" she asked. "I mean, I think it's great that you're questioning things, but you must have a lot on your mind right now."

"No, this is good. I need spiritual truth right now. Maybe it will even help me guide my mom in the right direction."

"Okay."

"So tell me more about theism and why it's different from pantheism."

"Well, theism says that God made all. Those who hold to this worldview include Christianity, Islam, and Judaism. God made the universe, but he is distinct from the universe. Pantheism says all is one and God is all. As we talked about as Rachel's, the largest religion that holds to this is Hinduism. Hinduism teaches that the ultimate reality is Brahman. There are different types of pantheism. The Greek philosopher Parmenides was the most rigorous pantheistic monist, arguing that everything is one.[65] Zen Buddhism teaches that there is oneness, like a life force, that permeates everything.[66] Shankara taught a version of absolute pantheism that said that God alone is real and anything else is unreal.[67] Radhakrishnan, on the other hand, believed in more of a multilevel pantheism by implying that God was the ultimate reality and that other things exist as less divine."[68]

"Whoa! Those are some crazy names. You're going to have to slow down with all of that name-dropping. What about Oprah and her friends? What do they believe about this stuff?"

"Well, it's hard to say, because none of them believe exactly the same thing. Sometimes they're inconsistent with their own teaching, too. But for the most part they hold to some type of pantheism that says 'all is God' and 'God is all.' They may use different terminology, but they believe that everything is ultimately God. 'You are God and the flower is God,' says the pantheist. For example, the other day I was reading Kathy Freston's book called *Quantum Wellness*. She said that however we choose to picture God, we are all connected to 'it.' She writes that we can call this Creative Force whatever we want: Jesus, Buddha, Allah, Divine Mother, or whatever feels right. She even said that an atheist may refer to a 'loving power.'"[69]

"That sounds okay to me. What's wrong with calling God by a different name? Why can't a person just believe that all is God or Pure Energy or Being or whatever they desire to call it?"

"Well, God can't be all of those things," Avatari commented.

"Why not?" asked Lindsey.

"Well, the God of the Bible has different characteristics than the god of Buddha, Allah, or a 'Divine Mother.' If there is only one God, he can't be all of those persons because they contradict each other. Remember what I was saying about truth?"

"Not really," Lindsey admitted.

"Anything opposed to the truth is false. Our minds may be limited, but our minds are not so limited that we can't know truth."

"How do you know that the truth is knowable? What if there are more than a billion people in the world who sincerely believe in some form of pantheism, whether it's Hinduism, Buddhism, or the spirituality of Oprah Winfrey? Would you say that all of their beliefs are false?" asked Lindsey.

"Their belief that 'all of us are God' is false. From the beginning of creation, one of Satan's greatest lies to Adam and Eve was that they would be 'like God.'[70] Remember, the truth about reality is true regardless of whether or not people believe that truth. In other words, even though over a billion people in the world may believe that 'God is all,' that doesn't make it true. We must be humble and honest enough to admit what is real and what is not."

"But it seems arrogant to say that you know what is true and what is real."

"Not necessarily. God meant for us to know that he is real. Because we're created in his image, God gave us a mind that has the potential to understand his revelation. A theologian named R. C. Sproul was once asked, 'What is the difference between the Christian God and the gods of other religions? The God of Christianity exists.'[71] The pantheist god, on the other hand, does not exist in reality."

"It just seems so arrogant when you say that pantheism and Oprah's beliefs about God are not true," Lindsey said, with a hint of disgust in her voice.

"Many people in our culture feel that it's arrogant to say another person's belief is not true, but really, don't you think it's arrogant for Oprah and her spiritual teachers, like Eckhart Tolle and Rhonda Byrne, to claim to be God or be part of God? The Bible says that Adam and Eve were faced with a temptation from Satan that would make them try to become like God, 'to know good and evil.' Yet Oprah and her spiritual teachers offer millions of people this same deception: that they are ultimately God. Our culture has attempted to redefine humility and tolerance to mean that you can't say that anybody else's beliefs are false. Even though they hide behind this mask of tolerance, they imply that anyone who disagrees with *their* belief is wrong. However, true humility is admitting that we are not God. God rebukes people in Scripture for thinking they are like God. In Psalms, God says, "You thought I was altogether like you. But I will rebuke you and accuse you to your face."[72] The only person who ever existed in the form of God is Jesus. The book of Philippians says that at the name of Jesus every knee should bow and every tongue should confess that Jesus Christ is Lord."[73]

"Many people in our culture feel it's arrogant to say another person's belief is not true, but really, don't you think it's arrogant for Oprah and her spiritual teachers to claim to be God or be part of God?"

"Okay, Av, I remember that verse from church, but many pantheists write about Jesus," replied Lindsey, her mind momentarily flashing to a picture of her mother lying in a hospital bed waiting for her.

"True," agreed Avatari. "But they redefine Jesus to fit their own pantheistic worldview. The other day I was browsing through Barnes & Noble and saw several best-selling books about spirituality. One that grabbed my attention was one about Jesus by Deepak Chopra. Barnes & Noble featured this book as one of the hardcover bestsellers of the month, so I was curious to look through it. In the book Chopra implies that by 'taking on God's identity'[74] and learning to trust yourself, you are trusting Jesus. You, Jesus, God, and the universe are one and the same. Immediately I realized that this book was not the gospel message taught by the Jesus I trust. Instead, it promoted the message of pantheism."

"Yeah, I remember as a teenager watching an episode of 'Oprah' with my mom. Shirley MacLaine was teaching a similar idea. She said that we were all god. And in *The Secret*, I remember Rhonda Byrne saying, 'We are One. We are all connected, and we are part of One Energy.'[75] So I can see why you'd say she's pantheistic," Lindsey said. "But Avatari, why do you think so many people are attracted to that philosophy?"

"For one, a lot of people think that they can 'add on' pantheism to whatever they already believe or they can 'add on' an additional spiritual belief to their previous worldview of pantheism. This is why many of my Hindu friends believe that they can accept Jesus and simply 'add him on' to their belief in thousands of other deities. Have you read C. S. Lewis's book *Miracles?*"

"No, I've read only read *The Chronicles of Narnia* and part of *Mere Christianity*."

"Well, Lewis suggested that pantheism catches on precisely because, like an old shoe, it is so comfortable.[76] Pantheism tells people the words they want to hear: 'You are good. You are infinite. You are God.'[77] I mean, naturally, we would rather hear someone say that than to hear someone like the apostle Paul say that we have fallen short of the glory of God and need a Savior named Jesus Christ to rescue us from the dominion of sin in our lives. Naturally we'd rather have Oprah empathize with our struggles and tell us how good we are rather than having Jesus tell us, 'Unless you humble yourselves and become like a little child, you will never enter the Kingdom of Heaven.'[78] We'd prefer to have spiritual teachers like Oprah's friends tell us to 'trust the truth within us' rather than hearing the words in Proverbs that say, 'He who trusts in himself is a fool.'"[79]

Lindsey shifted in her seat. "Wow, Av. I don't think I've ever heard you quite like this. You are getting bolder with your Christianity. But all of those verses seem to imply that we aren't good people, and we are. They make us feel bad about ourselves. Christianity seems to imply only negative thoughts about us."

"I know what you mean, but really, that's not the case," Avatari responded, her voice growing more passionate as she continued to speak. She knew that they would soon reach the hospital in Plano, and she wanted to be sure to leave Lindsey with a positive and true perspective on how much God loved her and her mom. "God did create humanity to be perfectly good. However, we have sinned. We have lied, made bad choices, been selfish, and, in general, lived for ourselves rather than God. Even though morally we are sinful, in another sense, we are very good, because we are created in the image of God. Jesus ultimately designed you and made no mistakes with your body or mind. Scripture says we are 'God's work of art.'[80] Another translation says, 'We are God's masterpiece.'[81] Each of us is a unique creation, one of a kind; and with God there is no shoddy workmanship—there is no junk! Because he lovingly created us and has ongoing plans for our lives, we can trust him. Another famous psalm by King David says,

> For it was You who created my inward parts;
> You knit me together in my mother's womb.
> I will praise You because I have been remarkably and
> wonderfully made.
> Your works are wonderful, and I know this very well.[82]

Avatari became even more impassioned as she continued. "Every person on the earth has a spiritual thirst for something that will satisfy. A philosopher once called it the 'God-shaped

78

void.' We may try to use a variety of worldly methods and quick fixes to fill that void, but only God's Spirit can truly satisfy.

"One of the similarities between pantheism and the teaching of Jesus is that God's immanent presence is in the world. God is here with us because he is Spirit, but contrary to what pantheism teaches, God is distinct from us. As we place our trust in Christ's work on the cross, God, who is transcendent and greater than us, fills us with the Holy Spirit. Even after God fills us with his Holy Spirit, we are still distinct beings from him. We have a relationship with Jesus and he certainly is our friend, but we are not the same person he is. Jesus says that God is still our 'Lord' and 'King.' Amazingly, this great and awesome God is ready to restore us to his favor and even call us his friends! Through Jesus we learn to connect with God in both spirit and truth. Jesus offers this relationship to any who will come to him. He says that if we are thirsty, we should come to him and he will give us freely the water of life.[83] Spiritually, he is talking about living life to the fullest because we have eternal life through his Spirit."

CHAPTER 8

Sixth Street Love

Is sin an illusion?

Avatari recognized Lindsey's struggle with her faith. She recalled the mixed feelings of joy and abandonment that she had experienced a couple of years earlier when she'd become a Christ follower. One of her most poignant memories was of defending her conversion to her father over the phone.

Two and half years earlier
Phone conversation between Austin, Texas, and New York, New York
"Avatari." She remembered hearing the disappointment that he'd laced with her name.

"Yes, Dad?"

"How could you betray us like this? You grew up with the teaching of the Bhagavad Gita, the Yoga Sutras, and the Upanishads. Even though your Americanized method of yoga was not our preference, we were so proud when you started teaching yoga to fellow students at Yale. But now you've betrayed us. How could you leave the faith of your family? This is just wrong of you!"

As painful as it had been to hear him regard her with such shame, she'd felt compelled to try to make him understand. "But Father, how can you say it is *wrong?* You once told me that Radhakrishnan said, 'Evil and error are not ultimate.' If moral rights and wrongs are illusions, like Radhakrishnan indicated, then why is my decision wrong?"[84]

"Don't talk back to me!" he bellowed. "I'm your father!"

The present
On the road to Plano

The sting of that painful conversation was still with Avatari, and as she looked over at Lindsey, she felt an overwhelming gratefulness that God was working in her friend's heart in a way that she had yet to see in the family that meant so much to her.

"Av? What are you thinking?" asked Lindsey.

"You know, it wasn't easy for me to completely trust in Jesus, Linds. At first, I felt an inexpressible joy about my relationship with God, but then I felt like I was going to literally throw up because I felt so lonely and so abandoned by my family. They have softened up some, but having my own father turn against me crushed my heart. Yet I still knew that becoming a Christian was the right thing to do. I understand that discussing spiritual or religious matters can be tough to do with family members, but I just want to let you know that I will be here to help answer questions about God the best I know how."

"Thanks, Av. What exactly inspired you to believe the God of the Bible was the real God?"

"One thing that got my attention was the conviction that God was the giver of absolute moral laws. I used to think that sin was an illusion. This is taught by many of the spiritual teachers that Oprah Winfrey endorses. When I was in college, I believed that good, evil, and morality were all just a matter of taste or opinion. If a student felt like practicing a particular sexual behavior outside of marriage, I thought there was nothing wrong with that. Their morals were just not the same as mine. But now I realize that I was not thinking correctly. Certain moral laws exist in nature that are absolute for all people."

"But Av, isn't morality something that is relative to the individual or culture? Wasn't there a philosopher who said, 'Man is the measure of all things'?"[85]

"Yes, there's been some debate about that statement made by the Greek philosopher Protagoras that was introduced to us by Plato's writings. Yet, if I were to meet Protagoras, I would probably ask him *which* man or person is the measure? Osama bin Laden or Gandhi? Adolf Hitler or Mother Teresa?" Avatari paused for a second to make sure Lindsey was in tune with the spiritual conversation. She knew that in about an hour and a half they would arrive at the hospital in Plano, and she wanted to be sensitive to the situation that Lindsey would face there.

Avatari continued, "Linds, I've become convinced that there is a moral standard outside these individuals that determines whose actions are right and wrong. That standard, which philosophers call natural law, cannot be us. This absolute natural law that is true for all people is written on the heart. As a soon-to-be lawyer, you know that laws imply that there is a lawgiver. I believe that God is the giver of the absolute moral law that applies to everybody."

Two and a half years ago
The University of Texas at Austin

"Professor Tanaka, do you have a second?" Avatari asked.

"Yes, Avatari, how can I help you?" The distinguished Asian professor leaned back in his chair and his wise eyes gave full attention to the young Indian lady.

"Well, this is my first semester at UT and I am really enjoying your class, but I wanted to ask you a question."

"Sure," he responded.

"Can there really be a single objective moral law that is true for all people, especially when there is more than one theory about it, coming from a variety of philosophers?"

"That's a good question, Avatari. But disagreement about the details does not prove that this law doesn't exist." He removed his glasses from the bridge of his nose and leaned forward as he explained, "The truth that there is an objective moral law or objective natural law is more important than any theories about it. The different theories of natural law *do* agree about the basic content. Many times, what they disagree about are secondary things, such as where the knowledge of it comes from."[86]

"Can there really be a single objective moral law that is true for all people, especially when there is more than one theory about it, coming from a variety of philosophers?"

Avatari nodded her head. "I see the validity in a moral absolute for all people, but this is contrary to what I've believed for most of my life—and it's definitely not something that's accepted by all my friends at Yale. Have you always known this natural law?"

"Ha! Good question. Yes, Avatari, but there were certainly times that I tried to deny its existence. When I graduated from Harvard, I wanted to teach ethics, philosophy, and politics, but I wanted to do it my own way. I used to tell my friends that we human beings just make up our own definitions of what's morally good and what's evil; and second, that you and I aren't responsible for what we do anyway. You see, during my student years at Harvard, I had ideas about spirituality and politics and had a self-centered form of so-called ethics became a kind of substitute religion. By the way, it's kind of like that in America for some political leaders today. Looking back now, I realize that deep down inside, I knew I had committed certain sins that I didn't want to repent of. But in the midst of my denial of moral absolutes, the presence of God made me very uncomfortable. Then I began studying famous atheists and searching for reasons that might show that God didn't exist, because I hated him. It was a miserable, lonely time in my life."[87]

"I see. But now you're a Christian and believe that there is a moral law that has been given by God, right? The other day in class, when speaking of Aquinas, did you mention a quote by C. S. Lewis?"

"Yes, I think I did mention Lewis."

"I loved reading *The Chronicles of Narnia* when I was kid. Didn't he give some easy-to-understand analogies for believing in a real right and wrong?"

"He did."

"If I want to get Lewis's thoughts on natural law, what book should I read?"

"Start with *Mere Christianity*," he said. He smiled and stood up to leave.

"Thanks," Avatari said. "I'll see you in class!"

Later that evening, Avatari purchased a copy of *Mere Christianity* at Barnes & Noble. After buying a venti latte at Starbucks, she settled down and began reading the first several chapters. She remembered Professor Tanaka saying that even though people disagree about certain aspects of the law of human nature, mankind has historically recognized this law.

She read the words of C. S. Lewis:

> Men have differed as regards to what people you ought to be unselfish to—whether it was only your own family, or your fellow countrymen, or everyone. But they have always

agreed that you ought not to put yourself first. Selfishness has never been admired. Men have differed as to whether you should have one wife or four. But they have always agreed that you must not simply have any woman you liked.[88]

As Avatari continued reading *Mere Christianity*, she reflected that perhaps there was a certain behavior determined by God for how she ought to live her life.

But the most remarkable thing is this. Whenever you find a man who says he does not believe in a real Right and Wrong, you will find the same man going back on this a moment later. He may break his promise to you, but if you try breaking one to him he will be complaining "It's not fair" before you can say Jack Robinson. A nation may say treaties don't matter; but then, the next minute they spoil their case by saying that the particular treaty they want to break was an unfair one. But if treaties do not matter, and there is no such thing as Right and Wrong—in other words, if there is no Law of Nature—what is the difference between a fair treaty and an unfair one? Have they not let the cat out of the bag and shown that, whatever they say, they really know the Law of Nature just like anyone else?[89]

Avatari began to look at the rationality that there was a real standard of right and wrong. *Every law has a lawgiver. There is a moral law; therefore, there's a moral lawgiver. The giver of this law is certainly not me.* She also reflected on a brief time during her sophomore year at Yale in which she clearly rejected the concept of a God who created the universe, because of the evil, suffering, and injustice that exists in the world. While reading Lewis, Avatari began to recognize that the author had gone through a similar journey and crisis of faith.

My argument against God was that the universe seemed so cruel and unjust. But how had I got this idea of just and unjust? A man does not call a line crooked unless he has some idea of a straight line. What was I comparing this universe with when I called it unjust.... Of course I could have given up my idea of justice by saying that the world was nothing but a private idea of my own. But if I did that, then my argument against God collapsed too—for the argument depended on saying that the world was really unjust, not simply that it did not happen to please my fancies.[90]

The present

Lindsey burst in, "But Avatari, this business of moral absolutes is so contrary to what Oprah says. I remember Eckhart Tolle saying that the mental labels of good and bad are ultimately illusory.[91] He said that if evil has any reality, then it's only relative, not absolute.[92] Couldn't good and evil just be relative?"

Avatari retorted, "Do you believe that racism or child sacrifice are absolutely wrong for all people in all cultures? Do you believe that it is only relatively wrong for a grown man to have sex with an animal or an innocent child?"

"This business of moral absolutes is so contrary to what Oprah says. I remember Eckhart Tolle saying that the mental labels of good and bad are ultimately illusory."

"Gross! Of course I believe those things are absolutely wrong!"

"Well, what's the basis? Who determines that the action is absolutely wrong for all people at all times?"

"Umm...I guess I see your point. I guess you want me to say the Bible?"

"I haven't mentioned the Bible, and I don't need the Bible to reveal the point I am making—that there are moral absolutes.

Certain behaviors such as racism, rape, incest, and other behaviors clearly go against the laws of nature."

"What? I thought Christians were supposed to quote the Ten Commandments."

"The Ten Commandments are one type of law written for the Jews. But I believe that the principles of the Ten Commandments are written on the hearts of all people. The Ten Commandments remind us of what is already written on our hearts. The apostle Paul wrote that those who did not receive the Old Testament or written law still had a law that was written on their hearts. He wrote in a letter to the church in Rome that those who do not have the law, do by nature things required by the law. They show that the requirements of the law are written on their hearts; their consciences are a good witness.[93] In other words, there is a law written on everybody's heart that reflects the principles of the Ten Commandments."

Is there a moral law written on my heart? Lindsey wondered, as her mind brought her to a memory she often wished she could forget.

Two years ago
Sixth Street Club in Austin, Texas

As Lindsey entered the Sixth Street Club with four of her friends, she noted the familiar smell of booze and sweat. A wave of depression washed over her. When she'd married Mark, she'd honestly thought that her clubbing days would be behind her. She could remember dreaming of dinner parties and hoping for a more stable family life with children. It was hard to believe that it turned out the way it had.

She drank the shot that her friend Katie handed her and allowed Miranda to drag her onto the dance floor. Bon Jovi's "Living on a Prayer" was playing loudly through the speakers. Lindsey resolved to shift her mood back to its earlier levity, not allowing herself to think anymore about Mark so she could thoroughly enjoy her night out with the girls.

"Hey! I know you!" A tall, dark-haired guy was standing in front of her, and in order to be heard he came incredibly close and shouted in her left ear. "Aren't you Mark Turner's wife?"

So much for not thinking anymore about Mark, Lindsey thought as she leaned back to get a good look at the guy's face. "Yeah." She looked down. "Well, I was—we're divorced," Lindsey yelled back. "How do I know you?"

She could feel his hand on her lower back this time as he leaned back in. "I used to play ball with Mark a couple years back. You used to watch from the stands. I never forget a pretty face. Too bad about Mark; he must have really lost his mind to let you go. Wanna dance?"

He's flirting with me! How long has it been since someone told me I'm pretty? "I thought we already were!" she quipped flirtatiously and bobbed in time with the music.

The night progressed speedily as she and Rob danced, drank, and flirted to song after song. She'd completely lost track of the time when she found herself pinned to the wall by the restroom with her fingers deep in his hair as he kissed her passionately.

The present

As she rode with Avatari to the hospital, Lindsey thought to herself how fitting it was that this buried memory would come to her now in the midst of their conversation about morality. She had dim memories of the cab ride to somewhere and even dimmer memories of all that followed. She remembered the strong taste of straight vodka at Rob's house. She remembered the feel of the carpet on her back and the smell of his breath after hours of fooling around. Mostly, though, she remembered the emptiness she felt when she opened her eyes in a strange room in the morning—feeling the sunlight streaming through an unfamiliar window and seeing a strange man sleeping beside her. She suddenly felt the memories of the night before rushing at her, and the flash of awareness that she was naked and lying next to a man she barely knew.

Lindsey had to admit that on that morning two years ago she'd known in her heart that what she'd done was wrong—and not just because the Bible told her so. Her conscience had told her so, and her heart had never let her forget. Her spirit ached with the shame of it. In her mind she knew that what Avatari had said was true.

CHAPTER 9

Will the Real Jesus Please Stand Up?

Is Jesus "the Jesus of Christ-consciousness"
or the Jesus of the New Testament?

Lindsey's head was reeling with questions about the true meaning of life and the sense of guilt she felt over her past sins. She began to relate all of this to her mother's situation. Her heart pounded heavily in her chest as she flipped open her cell phone and dialed her aunt's number.

"Hi, Aunt Susan. How's Mom?"

"Better, we think." Susan took a deep breath and exhaled into the phone's mouthpiece before continuing. "She hasn't woken up yet, Linds, but the doctors are taking really good care of her. They did confirm that it was an overdose. How are you holding up, sweetie?"

I feel like a scared little girl, thought Lindsey as she tried to keep the panic from creeping into her voice. "I'm doing okay—we're getting close to Plano now. Is there any way I could talk to her, Aunt Susan? Could you hold the phone to her ear for a second?"

"Let me check with the doctor..." Lindsey heard rustling and the sound of muffled voices before her aunt came back on the line. "Lindsey, they're still working on her and running some tests, but they said I could put you on speaker phone for just a second."

"Okay. Mom?" Lindsey said tentatively, recognizing the hollow echo of speaking to a room full of people. The lump that rose in Lindsey's throat when she called out to her mother took her by surprise. She felt a physical pain in her heart as tears stung her eyes. She was silent for a moment as she struggled to swallow enough to be able to manage, "I love you, Mom. I'm so thankful you're still alive! I'm going to be there in about forty minutes. Mom, I need you to hang on till I see you, okay?"

Lindsey heard the voices of nurses and people in the background until Susan picked up the phone and whispered, "Lindsey, the doctors need to concentrate on getting her vitals where they should be—keep driving safely, and we'll see you in a bit."

After hanging up, Lindsey looked at Avatari. "She's still not awake, Av. The doctors did confirm that she overdosed on painkillers. She's lucky to be alive. I can't believe my mother might be on the verge of...," her voice trailed off.

Not knowing quite what to say but wanting desperately to comfort her friend, Avatari simply said very softly, "We're almost there, Linds—you'll see her really soon."

In the silence that ensued, Lindsey began to consider how both she and her mother had struggled in recent years to figure out their spirituality. There had been a time when both of them had experienced some level of faith in the same God Avatari talked about, but she had to acknowledge that even before her father's death, they had somehow gotten off the path of that faith. Lindsey tried to process what had changed over the years and realized that, for her, it had begun to dissolve when she had stopped believing that the Jesus of the Bible *really* existed. Before that, she remembered asking him to come into her heart as a little girl and praying to him every night before she went to bed.

In recent years, Lindsey had maintained her spirituality, but her ideas about Jesus had changed. She had begun to believe in a Jesus similar to the one that Oprah and her spiritual teachers believed in. But now she was beginning to realize that the Jesus of Oprah and friends was different from the one portrayed in the books of Matthew, Mark, Luke, and John that she had read growing up.

While lifting up a fervent, silent prayer for her mother, Lindsey couldn't help but think that if there was ever a time to figure out if Christ was real and could perform miracles, it was now. Punching her iPhone, she googled the book she'd heard Marianne Williamson teach from, *A Course in Miracles*, that she adapted from Helen Schucman. She read:

> In most Christian religions, we were taught that we were born in sin (original sin) and that we are all sinners. We were also taught that Jesus saved us from the eternal fires of damnation by dying on the cross for our sins. In this crazy thought system, we made up a God that requires sacrifice of His Son to atone for our sins. When we really look at it with clarity, it would be quite a wild and crazy God that would have such a requirement to be appeased.[94]

In another place, Lindsey saw that *A Course in Miracles* said something similar: "How mad to think that you could be condemned, and that the holy Son of God can die!"[95]

Lindsey then remembered how Oprah had echoed these same thoughts in her online spiritual conversation with Eckhart Tolle. *Hmm*, Lindsey thought. *Oprah said that the purpose of Christ coming was not to die on the cross for our sins, but to show us the Christ-consciousness that we all have within us.*

"Avatari, I have a question about Jesus. I've always believed in him to some extent, but how do you know he was really God and that he really died? How can we ever know for sure that he resurrected?"

"I understand where you're coming from, Linds, and I think it's great that you're thinking through all of this. What's important to realize when you're asking these questions is that, although there are many conflicting answers, they can't all be true. Thankfully, we have many historical documents that reveal that we can know certain truths about Jesus in the same way we can know about any other historical figure. But that's me getting ahead of myself. Let me start by saying that God has always existed as one essence, but as three distinct persons: the Father, the Son, and the Holy Spirit."

"I have a question about Jesus. I've always believed in him to some extent, but how do you know he was really God and that he really died? How can we ever know for sure that he resurrected?"

"So you're saying that Jesus existed before he came to earth?" The idea sounded incredible to Lindsey.

"Yes. He is eternal in his divine nature. Paul wrote in a letter to the church at Colosse that Jesus existed before all things.[96] Jesus made similar claims about himself when he told a group of devout Jewish people, 'Before Abraham was, I AM.'[97] They laughed at him and said, 'You are not even fifty years old, and you claim that you know Abraham.' When Jesus made this claim of being the God who revealed himself to Moses, they picked up stones to try to kill him on the spot, but Jesus was able to escape."[98]

She continued, "It's impossible for us to completely understand everything about the nature of the infinite God. As humans, we'll never perfectly comprehend him, but we can certainly know him and apprehend certain characteristics of his being. This Trinity of unity and diversity within God has always been, but two thousand years ago Christ took on a nature of humanity and came to this earth as the person of Jesus. God became like us through the person of Jesus."

"Can we really know that for sure, though?" asked Lindsey.

"Yes, with certainty beyond a reasonable doubt we have enough evidence to place our faith in him. Many of the spiritual teachers that Oprah recommends will attack this belief and say you can't know that much about God. If you claim to know certain characteristics about God, these new spiritual teachers may mock you and say that in your limited mind, you can't know these attributes of God. They will say that knowledge is non-essential and all we have to do is 'be.' Yet, even though they may make fun of those who claim to have knowledge of God's true nature, they're also claiming to have true knowledge in regard to God's nature when they say that particular attributes of his nature are unknowable. So, can we have knowledge of certain truths about who God is? Yes! God, in his love for us, has given us a mind to be able to understand these truths. He is passionate about wanting to have a personal relationship with you, and he has preserved evidence to show that Christ did die in history and was raised from the dead."

"Yeah," Lindsey replied, hating her doubt, "but that's just a claim from the Bible."

"When we look at the individual documents of the New Testament, we should examine their reliability like any other historical work of antiquity. Even if we were to get rid of the New Testament and look at non-Christian sources that mention Jesus, we could confirm his existence. He was noted by Josephus, Celsus, Tacitus, the Jewish Talmud, and a handful of other historical sources, all totally apart from the Bible. We know that

Jesus lived during the time of Tiberius Caesar, that he was a wonder-worker who claimed to be the Messiah, and that his disciples believed that he rose from the dead. We also know from these sources outside the New Testament that Christianity spread rapidly, as far as Rome, because his followers believed that Jesus had died and come back to life. Historical data shows that they denied the Roman gods and worshipped Jesus as God. They were so convinced of what they had seen, they were willing to die for this belief."[99]

"I used to believe that Jesus came to die," Lindsey replied, knowing she sounded sad and dejected, but finding herself without the energy to rise above it. "But *A Course in Miracles* said that it was crazy for us to believe in such a thing. That Eckhart guy said the same thing. What do you think, Av?"

"I don't think it's crazy at all, because of all the historical evidence of his existence and death. However, I understand a little where they're coming from in a theological sense. Even I admit that, to some extent, it seems really 'out there' that a perfect Being who never gets lonely or insecure would love us so much that he would take our punishment. *A Course in Miracles* is clearly false in saying that we made this system up, though. There's just too much historical evidence that Christ lived on earth, claimed to be God, and died on the cross to rescue us from hell."

"Avatari, do you really believe in hell? I have so much trouble believing that a loving God would let anyone go to a place like that—I'd much rather believe we all go to heaven." Lindsey knew that what she was saying was not in line with how Avatari felt, but something inside her was pushing for answers. She was tired of being so unsure all the time.

"I know this is a sensitive subject for you right now, Linds—I can't even imagine what you're going through. I think it breaks God's heart that some people would rather be separated from him, but if you think everybody is going to go to heaven, that means that you also think unrepentant people like Hitler, racists, rapists, murderers, and child molesters who show hatred toward God and other humans will all be in heaven. Are you okay with that?"

Lindsey hesitated. "Hmm . . . I don't know."

"God's holiness demands justice. We are separated from him because of our sins, but his mercy offers forgiveness. Yes, God loves us. One of my favorite verses says, 'But God demonstrated his love for us in that while we were still sinners Jesus Christ died for us.'[100] As a Baptist, don't you remember that verse in John's Gospel that says, 'For God so loved the world that he gave his only begotten Son that whosoever believes in him shall not perish but have everlasting life?"[101]

Hearing Lindsey's questions and sensing her desperation for satisfying answers, Avatari remembered a time when she was looking for the same affirmations in her spiritual search.

Two and a half years earlier
Campus Christian Outreach, Austin, Texas

Avatari thought to herself, *They've been singing this "Let it Rain" song for almost half an hour! The first time around it sounded like a nice enough song, but at this point it seems like they're trying to build up some kind of spiritual experience.* They'd been standing in the auditorium for the past thirty minutes, and by now Avatari was seriously regretting giving Campus Christian Outreach a try. *And what's the deal with those nerdy guys staring at the girls in the front row who are being extra dramatic by raising their hands? This whole thing is creeping me out.*

At the end of the drawn-out song, the campus minister stood up and offered to answer any questions or pray with those who felt the tug of God's Spirit. *I am not sure if I should ask my question, but since I'm not here to impress anyone, I might as well give it a try.* Avatari tentatively raised her hand. The minister pointed to her. She heard herself say, "Hi. I am not a Christian, but I consider myself spiritual. As I am learning about other religions, I am curious about the evidence and importance of believing in the virgin birth of Christ."

Hoping to find an answer to the probability of a miracle occurring or some historical evidence for such an event, Avatari listened intently to the campus pastor's disappointing response.

"Faith is all you need," he said. "Just believe! We came here to experience the presence of God." After a question about some John Calvin guy, the group went back to singing the same worship songs, including "Let it Rain" again.

Frustrated with what seemed like emotional manipulation, Avatari actually prayed awkwardly, "God, please let it rain so these Christians will stop singing the same words over and over and I can leave without anyone noticing me!"

Two weeks after Avatari's unpleasant experience at the Campus Christian Outreach, a fellow student named Lisa, whom she met in a course on existentialism, told her about an upcoming lecture and promised her that the guest lecturer at the Campus Christian Outreach would be excellent. Born in India, Dinesh D'Souza was a graduate of Cornell and served as a research scholar at Stanford University.

At first Avatari was a little hesitant to return to the Campus Christian Outreach, but after checking out some of his credentials, Avatari figured that it was at least worth giving the spiritual gathering another chance, even if this Dinesh guy seemed a little more conservative than she preferred. After hearing complex cosmological arguments for the existence of God and a case for the supernatural, this obviously bright man spoke of the simplicity and uniqueness of the Christian message. He said:

> Religion in general is man's strategic manual to reach God. But Christianity is not a religion in this sense. Christianity holds that man, no matter how hard he tries, cannot reach God. Man cannot ascend to God's level because God's

level is too high. Therefore there is only one remedy: God must come down to man's level. Scandalous though it may seem, God must, quite literally, become man and assume the burden of man's sins. Christians believe that this was the great sacrifice performed by Christ. If we accept Christ's sacrifice on the basis of faith, we will inherit God's gift of salvation. That's it. That is the essence of Christianity.[102]

As she listened to this intriguing speaker, Avatari began to realize his message was starting to make sense. *This has to be true. I know it's true that I've been sinful. I've lied, lusted, been selfish and materialistic... God, now that I have heard the truth, do I even have a choice? I need Christ. But what will my family think if I place my trust in Jesus? Am I sure I want to do this?*

Professor D'Souza continued talking about how one obtained this salvation.

How, then, are we to have salvation? For most religions, man must take the active role. Hinduism and Buddhism offer solutions that are remarkably similar: Through meditation we confront our selfish desires and recognize the "self" is the core of the problem. So we strive, in various ways, to eliminate this self and achieve its extinction. In effect, we seek to become nothing. We can advance toward this goal not merely through meditation but also through disciplined self-renunciation: renunciation of possessions, renunciation of sensual pleasure, and so on. This is a supremely difficult process.... Judaism and Islam offer a different formula, although they lead their adherents down the same path. Judaism and Islam are religions of law. Both have elaborate rituals and codes: Pray five times a day. Pack up and go to Mecca. Sacrifice a lamb or a goat. Wear a long beard.... Christianity raises the bar even higher than other religions by insisting that in order to enter God's kingdom we must be perfect. Not good, but perfect. ... So how can a salvation be reconciled with divine holiness and justice? The Christian answer is that God decided to pay the price himself for human sin.... Thus, through the extremity of Golgotha, Christ reconciles divine justice and divine mercy and provides man with a passport to heaven. The bridge man was unable to build to God, God has built for man. ... So what's the difficulty? The difficulty is in realizing that we are sinful and that there is nothing we can do to solve this problem.[103]

As D'Souza spoke, Avatari admitted that she wanted to know Jesus Christ. Not just as some ancient religious guy but as a real person who overcame death in history. Because of his death, she longed to unload all her sins through what he did on the cross. Avatari fought the tears that filled her eyes, but found she couldn't hold them back as her heart said the words that would change her life. *Jesus, forgive me. I trust in you.* After her prayer she felt kind of sick, but she realized that the spiritual battle she'd been fighting both intellectually and emotionally had now resolved itself. God loved her. She was his.

CHAPTER 10

Reincarnation or Resurrection?

*What happens to the soul and
body after death?*

While Avatari was lost in the memory of that Campus Christian Outreach years ago, Lindsey had allowed her mind to wander too. She had been thinking about her father. Since he had passed away, she had often experienced the flash of a memory from an Easter Sunday when she was a child. She remembered excitedly bounding down the stairs in her new pink Easter dress, calling out for her dad to come and see her. She recalled twirling in the kitchen, proudly showing her daddy how the skirt whirled around her, and then pointing out the frill on the lacy white socks that her mother had bought for her to wear with her white patent Mary Janes.

Lindsey remembered looking up at her father, eager for his approval. She had felt such a rush of love and pleasure when her father said, "You're so beautiful!" It was a sweet memory that never failed to bring her peace when she thought of it. Tears came to her eyes now as she considered what she and Avatari had been talking about. She yearned for the reassurance that she would see her father again one day.

"Avatari, what do you think heaven is like?" Lindsey asked while noticing raindrops beginning to fall on the windshield. "A lot of these 'New Thought' gurus say that we cease to exist as individuals, while merging back into the universal life force. I remember Marianne on 'Oprah' kind of implying that the resurrection was more like a state of mind. She said that the message of the resurrection is that 'the crucifixion never occurred, except in our minds.'[104] Of course, Eckhart told Oprah that he doesn't even think about it. What do you think, Avatari? Does the afterlife matter? I really want to see my father again."

"It really does matter. God has made it possible for you to see your dad again. Jesus said that those who trust in him will go to a place called heaven. Heaven is a physical and spiritual place, not just a state of mind. The passages from the Bible describe heaven as a place filled with joy, excitement, pleasure, and activity. Knowing your father's faith, I believe that he is with Jesus right now... probably with billions of other people."

"But how do you know for sure? As a philosopher, you've heard so many other ideas and spiritual beliefs about the immortality of the soul."

"Well, there certainly are a lot of theories about what happens after one dies. There have been debates about both what happens to the soul and what happens to the body."

"Well, what are the different views?" asked Lindsey.

"Hmm... let me start with Socrates." Taking a sip of her water, Avatari seemed to be setting her mind on the topic at hand. "As one of the wisest men to ever live, he certainly had confidence when he faced death that his soul would live. Yet he and his brilliant student Plato had a little bit more of a negative view toward the human body. Let me put it this way. Some of the followers of Plato held such a high view of the soul that they thought the body was more like a prison. If you die, your soul escapes like a bird flying out of a cage. As a Christian, I agree with Socrates to some extent. I believe the soul lives on not because it is immortal, but because God allows us to live. Yet I also hold that our body will be raised to life."

"Don't a lot of spiritual teachers say that our souls live on?" Lindsey asked as she watched the raindrops pelting the windshield. She hoped the shift in weather wouldn't slow them down, but felt somehow that the dreariness better suited her heart-heavy mood.

"Yes, they do. Many of the pantheistic Eastern religions like Hinduism teach that our souls exist but they are reincarnated. My parents still hold to their belief in reincarnation. Some of the other Eastern pantheistic forms of spirituality that have been adapted from Buddhism teach that our individuality ceases to exist after our souls are absorbed into Oneness. It seems that many of these so-called spiritual teachers that Oprah recommends are basically saying the same thing. Yet, on the other hand, there have been many naturalistic philosophers and scientists who say that humans are only physical. They say the human body is all we are and what some refer to as an 'immaterial soul' doesn't even exist. Once your body dies, that's all there is. No afterlife. No miraculous resurrection of the body. No heaven. That's it. Um, I feel like I've been rambling a lot about religion."

"No. I want to know. What about the religions that believe God created the universe?"

"Well, as far as Eastern theistic religions, Muslims believe in paradise. Also, in the days of Jesus, most Jewish spiritual teachers believed that when you died your soul would live on, but they also believed that your body would someday be raised to life. Unlike some of the Eastern pantheistic religions, they held that the body was sacred and would be supernaturally raised to life in the end."

"Really?" Lindsey asked.

"Yeah, many of the Eastern pantheistic religions that didn't hold the physical in such a high regard would cremate the body so it would just 'return to the earth.' But the Jews would bury bodies with a sense of honor and sacredness, with the expectation that one day those bodies would be brought back to life. They were so dogmatic about their beliefs in the resurrection of the body that they would often get into heated debates with another sect of Jews who didn't believe in the resurrection."

"I see. Does it really matter one way or the other?" Lindsey asked.

"I think it does matter. If God, the Eternal Being, exists as the one who created us in his image and likeness, then I believe he created us to last forever. Jesus told his disciples on many occasions about a real place called heaven."

"Well, with all of these different views of the afterlife, how can I know for sure what Jesus taught was true?"

"We can trust Jesus not *just* because of what he said, but because of what he did. Don't get me wrong—what he said was extremely important. He told his disciples that he was going to heaven to get a place ready for them. After Thomas asked him how they could get to this place of heaven, Jesus answered by saying that he was *the way* and then he added, 'Because I live, you also will live.' These teachings of Christ were unique compared to those of any other spiritual teacher, because not only did he speak of the afterlife, but he said that our decision about what we believe about him influences our destiny. On one occasion, before he performed an extraordinary miracle by raising his friend Lazarus from the dead, he said, 'I am the resurrection and the life. He who believes in me will live, even though he dies.'[105] In other words, he allows us to make the decision to trust in him for this everlasting life." Avatari paused and looked at Lindsey.

She continued, "But the true uniqueness of what makes Jesus so different is that he didn't just *speak* about the afterlife, he *demonstrated* it. Jesus gave us proof! He physically rose again from the grave. You see, up until that point some of the Jewish spiritual leaders thought that after they died, God would one day supernaturally raise their bodies back to life. But they had no evidence, no way to verify this. Of course, they were shocked when this guy shows up claiming to be the great 'I AM' who appeared to Moses, saying that he was 'the way' to heaven, that he was 'the resurrection and the life.' Jesus was telling them that, because he lives and overcame death, he will also supernaturally raise our bodies from the dead and transform them in the future."

"So, Avatari, you're saying that this physical bodily resurrection is very important. What's your evidence that Jesus actually died and came back?"

"Before the resurrection can take place, we first must find evidence that Christ died on the cross. A few critics have tried to say that perhaps he didn't die to begin with. Let me just say that the Roman soldiers were experts in execution. They made sure they got the job done, or they paid with their life! I once read in a *Journal of the American Medical Association* about some doctors who documented the impossibility of a victim surviving a Roman execution.[106] If people have doubts whether a human could survive the brutality of a Roman execution, they just need to read a couple of history books or watch five minutes of the movie *The Passion of the Christ*. Even a liberal scholar of the Jesus Seminar, John Dominic Crossan, admitted, 'That he was crucified is as sure as anything historical can be.'[107] Jesus was brutally beaten, flogged with a cat-o'-nine-tails tearing his flesh, hung on a cross with thick spikes driven through his hands and feet, then—to ensure that he was dead—a Roman soldier pierced Jesus in the side. After Jesus died, historically we have early documentation that the tomb he was buried in, which belonged to the respected Jewish leader Joseph of Arimathea, was in fact discovered to be empty. In a book that I recently read by Dr. William Lane Craig, a leading expert on the resurrection, he writes that the empty tomb story is part of very old source material used by Mark. Also, this old information was transmitted by Paul in 1 Corinthians 15. And then the fact that the women's testimony was not considered admissible in court in first-century Palestine counts in favor of the women's role in discovering the tomb."[108]

"Hold on. If I get what you are telling me correctly, you are saying that the resurrection was documented very early?"

"Yes, it was documented within just a few years."

"Well, tell me more about the women. That's stupid that the women's testimony wasn't allowed in court during those days," commented Lindsey as she watched lit-up skyscrapers passing by.

"Throughout history, people may have died for a lie, but they thought it was true. People do not die for a lie that they know to be false. People die for what they think to be true."

"Well, the very fact that the faithful and brave women discovered the body of Jesus before the scared disciples did indicates this is what really happened. If the male disciples were just making this story up, they would not have specifically said that the women discovered the empty tomb before them. That would have been embarrassing for them in their culture."

"I never thought about that, but it makes sense. Can you tell me some more evidence? I want to know that these appearances were not just experienced by a few people."

"Well, I mentioned that scholars date the 'creedal' section of 1 Corinthians 15 between two and eight years after Christ's resurrection. Paul then notes the specific people that Jesus appeared to. He also adds that Jesus appeared to over five hundred brothers at one time! Now, as significant as the number five hundred is, what's even more important is the next fact that Paul writes. Paul said, 'Most of them remain to the present, but some have fallen asleep.'[109] In other words, Paul was saying that if you do not believe my testimony about the resurrection, then check it out with the eyewitnesses—hundreds of eyewitnesses of the resurrection are still alive."

"Okay. Avatari, with everything that has gone on in my life, when I think about this evidence of the resurrection, I really feel in my heart and mind that it's true. But suppose I were to play devil's advocate and say, 'How do we know that these eyewitnesses weren't just making the story up?'"

"Good question! When Jesus was arrested by the Roman guards, the disciples were terrified and fled for their lives. Peter denied Jesus three times that evening. A teenage servant girl approached Peter and said, 'You look like one of his disciples.' Peter, being scared for his life, began to curse at her and said, 'I don't know what you are talking about.' However, a few days later, something changed in the life of Peter. He went from being a timid coward in front of a servant girl to a bold witness as he courageously stood up in front of three thousand people and proclaimed the resurrection of Jesus. What happened?"

"Um . . . I guess Peter actually saw Jesus?" Lindsey said, drawing on her years of Sunday school for the answer.

"You're right! Peter *saw* a man who was dead come back to life! After the resurrection, eleven out of twelve of the apostles were martyred—and not just because of something they believed in. They were martyred for something that they *fervently thought to be true.*"

"But haven't lots of weird cult people died for a lie?"

"Throughout history, people may have died for a lie, but they thought it was true. People do not die for a lie that they know to be false. People die for what they think to be true. I heard this philosophy professor named Dr. Kreeft ask something like, 'Why would the apostles lie? . . . If they lied, what was their motive, what did they get out of it? What they got out of it was misunderstanding, rejection, persecution, torture, and martyrdom.'"[110]

"I understand," Lindsey said, nodding fervently in agreement. "But is it possible that what the disciples saw was just a spiritual resurrection that was nonphysical? Couldn't they have just seen the spirit of Jesus visiting them, like a ghost?"

"If it didn't take place physically, then Jesus didn't conquer death. The accounts tell us that, on several occasions after his death, Jesus ate food with his disciples. He also reached out his nail-pierced hands and said 'touch me' to prove that he was physically raised from the dead. The apostle Paul told the church at Corinth that this bodily resurrection is the foundation of the Christian faith. Paul said that if there wasn't a resurrection of the dead, then all of his teaching and preaching we have in the New Testament was a waste. He also wrote in 1 Corinthians that if Christ has not been raised, then our spiritual faith is useless, we are all a bunch of liars, we are still unforgiven in our sins, and we are to be pitied more than anybody else!"[111]

"Oh my!" Lindsey had to think about that for a few moments. "I think I feel comfortable believing that Jesus' resurrection was real, but what does all this mean for where my dad is now?"

"He is with Jesus in soul, but one day his body will supernaturally be transformed and brought back to life."

"That just seems so far out to me! How can you say it's reasonable to believe that all the human bodies that have died will one day be physically changed and brought back to life?"

"Lindsey, you believe in God, so don't you believe that miracles are possible?"

"Well, yeah, I guess so."

"I believe that the greatest miracle is creation," said Avatari. "When we think about God creating the world, it's so amazing. God made something out of nothing! Previously, no physical matter existed, and then God spoke and *bang!* Instantly, matter, light, and energy existed in time and space. Also, if God created the heavens, he can certainly make us a home in heaven."

"I guess I don't see the connection between miracles, creation, and heaven," commented Lindsey.

"If God has the power to create something out of nothing, then it's no problem for him to perform other miracles. If God created the water, it's not a problem for him to walk on water. If God created human beings, then he certainly has the power to bring dead humans back to life."

"You know, Av, that makes a lot of sense. I never thought about it all being intertwined like that, but when I think about the change in the lives of the early Christians, I can tell that they died not just for something they believed, but for something they actually saw. I can see that if God was the one to create life then it makes sense to believe in the resurrection of Jesus—and that his resurrection gives me evidence that I'll see my dad one day in heaven when we're both raised."

As she spoke, Lindsey realized that she really did believe everything Avatari had been explaining to her. She immediately asked God to cleanse her of her sins and trusted in Jesus' death and resurrection. After her prayer, she thought of her dad and that memory of him watching her dance happily in her Easter dress. For the first time since his death, she had spiritual hope, knowing she would see him again. "I just hope I get the chance to share this beautiful message with my mom," she said.

"I've been praying nonstop that you will, Linds," Avatari said. She made the left turn into the hospital parking lot. "We're here now... are you ready to go inside?"

CHAPTER 11

Watching "Oprah" on Vacation

*How can people experience the
love of God through Jesus?*

The smell of sickness and sterility was all around her. Lindsey suddenly regretted asking Avatari to stay in the waiting room. She stood, feeling very alone, in the door frame of her mother's hospital room, hardly believing that she was really back in this frightening place again.

Lindsey had grown accustomed to these sounds and routines during her father's illness, but now it was her mom—who had always seemed so whole and warm—who barely made a lump under the blankets on the bed in front of her. *This is my mother. My mother is dying.* The reality of it hit Lindsey hard, and she hurried to her mom's bedside.

Barbara's face was pale and she had tubes stemming from her nose and arms. Her hair was matted messily around her head. "Oh, Mom!" Lindsey moaned softly, her face crumpling as she leaned over to embrace her mom. Her hand found her mother's and her head hit the mattress, where she buried her face in the stiff hospital sheets.

As she embraced her mom, her heart unloaded itself and she bawled like a child. Hearing deep sounds erupt from hollow parts of her, she gripped her mother's hand with a fierce intensity. Her mind raged. Coherent thought was beyond her as she begged from the deepest recesses of her soul, *Please, God! Don't take her from me.*

"Lindsey?" It was barely a word, but fully a breath, and all of a sudden the world shifted.

"Mom? Mom, are you awake?" Lindsey stood up in astonishment, not daring to believe that she'd heard her name.

"I'm so thirsty," Barbara croaked dryly.

Lindsey's relief was profound as she accepted that her deepest fear and sorrow no longer had a place. She brushed a lock of hair from her mother's forehead and witnessed her struggle to refocus her eyes and regain awareness. There was a distinct moment where unconsciousness met clarity and Barbara's eyes filled with tears. She looked up at Lindsey and quickly averted her eyes as a single tear dropped from her lid, slid along the side of her face, and landed on the pillow beside her ear. Lindsey buzzed the nurse and requested some crushed ice.

After patiently waiting to talk until the nurse left, Lindsey finally let it out. "Why? Don't you know how much I love you?

> *She gripped her mother's hand with a fierce intensity. Coherent thought was beyond her as she begged from the deepest recesses of her soul,* Please, God! Don't take her from me.

Do you know how badly you just scared me? What would I do without you, Mom? What were you thinking?" Lindsey raged and pleaded in a single sentence, all her hurt and fear pouring out before the concern and gentleness she'd intended could surface.

Her mother's forehead furrowed and she blushed with shame. "I don't know what I was thinking. I can never tell you how sorry I am for scaring you like that, Lindsey. I don't know how I'll ever make this right." Her head slumped to the side and sobs shook her shoulders. After a minute, a plea for understanding seemed to escape, without purpose but ringing of bitter truth. "I was just so lonely without your dad."

"Oh, Mom. I'm so sorry," Lindsey said with tears in her eyes. She took both her hands and brought her mother's face up so their chins were level. It took a second before Barbara allowed their eyes to meet, and when they did Lindsey spoke with a conviction and clarity of soul that she was only coming to terms with in that instant. Her strength came from somewhere deep, and the assuredness in her voice both took her by surprise and reaffirmed her confidence in the belief she'd claimed in the car with Avatari.

"Mom, both of us have been so discouraged lately. I wanted to be strong for you, and I know how badly you wanted Daddy back. But I believe God wants us to trust him." She continually wiped at her mother's tears with her thumbs as they fell. "The thing is, Mom, it was Daddy's faith in Jesus that kept him strong. It was God. I think we've both drifted from trusting God."

Lindsey stopped for a moment. She wanted to allow her words to sink in and wanted to be sure she wasn't overwhelming her mother so soon after waking up. She could see, though, that her mom was waiting for her to continue and she felt compelled to go on.

"Daddy believed so fully that God was real. I took it for granted that he loved Jesus so much. It wasn't just a Sunday morning thing with him. When I used to get up early to go running, I would see Dad in his office, around five thirty in the morning, on his knees. He was praying for you and me. He didn't always know I was listening, but I was. Mom, you know that I've tried so hard to run from this message of the Christian faith. But Dad had confidence that Jesus gave himself so that we can experience a real relationship with him."

"Lindsey, I haven't heard you talk this way about God since you were a little girl. What's going on?" Barbara asked her daughter in disbelief.

"Mom, I've been really seeking truth spiritually and asking Avatari a lot of questions. I've realized in talking to her that while God is completely good, he is always completely God. We can't make him into whatever we want him to be, to suit our own purposes or understanding. The creation of the universe and the Bible show us who he really is. It's in our own ignorance and unwillingness to understand his perfect justice that we attempt to re-create him into a sentiment, an idea, a force, a hope, a feeling . . . a secret."

She took a deep breath and continued. "Just awhile ago, I repented of my sins and trusted the real Jesus for dying for me. After talking with Avatari, I am convinced I need him to guide me and give me wisdom, because my methods aren't working and what I've been reading in these 'spiritual' books isn't helping. I'm hoping this is a journey we can take together, Mom. I believe that if we do, we'll see Daddy again, when the time comes. And Mom—it has to be in God's time, not ours."

Barbara's tears had stopped and she shook her head slightly as a small smile appeared on her face. "It's unbelievable how much like your father you are, Lindsey. He'd be so proud of you right now." Her hand came up to meet Lindsey's on her cheek, and their eyes locked. She said with conviction, "You're right. We forgot God. We've gone our own way. Let's follow your dad's example."

Mother and daughter embraced and rocked back and forth for a while on the bed, comforting each other with their words and laughing at the occasional memory that they shared. They talked about the past few months and the ways they'd tried to reach out to each other and how nothing had seemed to go right. Then Lindsey felt inspired and asked her mom something she wouldn't have dreamed of asking her just days before. "Mom, could I bring Avatari in here? I'd love for her to pray with us. She's really been such a rock for me through everything. She has helped me to understand truth and God. Could we all pray together?"

With her mother's blessing, Lindsey ran out to the waiting room, where she found Avatari sitting on an orange hospital chair with her hands folded and her head bent. Her eyes were closed, so it wasn't until Lindsey laid her hand on her shoulder that she looked up. Concern was etched on her face, but her expression quickly altered when she heard Lindsey's lighthearted tone and good news request. Back in the hospital room, the three ladies joined hands in a circle—Avatari on one side of Barbara and Lindsey on the other—and although Avatari had offered to pray, it was Lindsey's voice that asked for help and healing.

"Dear Father in heaven, we need you. My heart has been so full of distress, but it's now filled with thankfulness for who you are and for giving us another chance. We thank you for the death and resurrection of Christ. I thank you so much that you spared my mother's life today. I will always be grateful for the time of healing we were able to have and that I got the chance to share with her how much I love her—and, more important, how much you love her. I thank you for Avatari too, God. She is so strong in her belief and lives with such peace and is such an example of you. Thank you for putting her in my life as a guide to help me understand truth. And thank you, Father, most of all, for your incredible love. Lord, please forgive me of my past.

Help me resist the urge to compromise your truths to accommodate my desires. Help me to live in such a way that others see in me what I saw in Avatari. Thank you, Father, for forgiving me and giving me another chance."

Seven months later
Miami, Florida
"Gosh, I hope it clears up today. It's been raining for the last two days, and I'm still as pale as I was when we got here," complained Lindsey.

"Honey, just try to enjoy the time off! You girls are going to be so busy with your new jobs you may not be able to join me at the beach house for a while," Barbara replied as she laid some fresh fruit on the table in front of the girls.

"Why don't we go to the mall this afternoon if it doesn't clear up?" suggested Avatari.

"Yeah, I need to get out. It doesn't seem right to spend vacation in front of the television," Lindsey said as she flipped through the channels. She landed on one and Oprah's voice filled the room.

"Boy, it's been a while since I've heard that voice," commented Barbara.

"Yeah, it's been a while for me, too," replied Lindsey. "Do you not watch her anymore, Mom?"

"Months ago, when I started devoting more of my time to prayer and Scripture memory, I decided not to watch her as much," said Barbara. "She's had so many good programs, but it seemed to me that recently she'd developed a spiritual agenda that was contrary to the Bible. I felt like it was a negative influence on my walk with Christ. Oprah said she was opening our minds, but I think that really contributed to my confusion about what I believed. I felt like I needed to stop watching her altogether for a while and regroup. Avatari, you don't watch 'Oprah' anymore, do you?"

"Well, actually, I still watch her some, but not as much as I used to because I have been so busy. I keep up with her because I still get *O Magazine*."

"So you haven't boycotted her show, Lindsey?" Barbara asked.

"No, I haven't boycotted her altogether. I don't have much time to watch her show, but like Avatari, I do sometimes read her magazine or check out her website. I have actually just prayed for Oprah recently." After Lindsey mentioned her prayer for Oprah, she remembered something that she wrote in her prayer journal a few nights earlier:

> *Dear Heavenly Father, I want to thank you for the work you have done in my life. My desire is that Oprah would see that when you are described as "jealous," that term means that you are passionate about a relationship with her. God, you love her, just like you love all of us. But you are also perfectly just, and you call us to repentance and to worship you in spirit and in truth. My hope is that she will turn to your Son, the true Jesus of the New Testament, not the Jesus of Eckhart Tolle or Marianne Williamson. I thank you, God, that your Son died for our sins. With all of Oprah's potential for influence, I think it would do the world a lot of good if she would turn to you and proclaim your true Son.*

After briefly reminiscing about her prayer journal entry, Lindsey hit the power button on the TV to turn it off. She looked out the window and said to the others, "Hey, it looks like the sun is coming out..."

Discussion Questions

These questions are suggested to help guide friendly discussion in home community groups, book clubs, and Sunday school Bible classes.

Discussion I: Chapters 1–3

1. Do you watch "Oprah"? If not, who is someone close to you that watches "The Oprah Winfrey Show"? *I KNOW THERE ARE PEOPLE BUT NO ONE SPECIFIC.*

2. Oprah didn't feel right about God being jealous, but Avatari suggests that God's jealousy is not the same as human jealousy. What were the reasons Avatari gave? *GOD IS JEALOUS FOR US WHEN WE SERVE OTHER "GODS" WEALTH, PEOPLE, ETC*

3. Could jealousy ever be used for good? How so? What analogy did Avatari give? *WHEN WE CHASE AFTER THINGS THAT AREN'T GOOD FOR US / WIFE'S JEALOUSY OF HUSBAND'S UNFAITHFULNESS.*

4. Avatari shares that God's jealousy is combined with God's love. What are some characteristics that Avatari says she discovered about God's love? *IT TAKES THE INITIATIVE (PG 27) GOD IS PASSIONATE ABOUT A RELATIONSHIP WITH US.*

5. Oprah believes that there are many paths to what she calls God. She doesn't believe that Jesus is the only way. What biblical teaching might contract this thinking? *I AM THE WAY, THE TRUTH & THE LIGHT NO ONE COMES TO THE FATHER BUT BY ME. JOHN 14:6*

6. Read John 14 and Acts 4. How do you think Oprah would respond to these two chapters? *I REALLY DON'T KNOW HOW SHE WOULD RESPOND. I'M SURE IT WOULD BE SOMETHING BIZARRE. PROOF IS PG 35*

Discussion II: Chapters 4–5

1. How does Avatari define religious pluralism? Avatari makes a distinction between two types of pluralism. How do they differ? *AS "RELIGIOUS" OR SPIRITUAL" THE NEW TYPE OF PLURALISM TEACHES THAT YOU MUST ACCEPT cov NOT JUST TOLERATE DIFFERENCES.*

THEM AS TRUE OR VALID

2. Avatari mentioned that even though the "new religious pluralism" is touted as open-mindedness, it's rather just another type of exclusivism. How is that possible? *BECAUSE THEY DON'T ACCEPT WHAT I BELIEVE AND THAT I DON'T ACCEPT THEIR BELIEF.*

3. Oprah and Eckhart seem to indicate that beliefs are not important. What did Jesus in the New Testament say about the relationship between salvation and belief? *THAT GOD REQUIRES US TO BELIEVE IN THE ONE HE HAS SENT.*

4. Avatari shows that even though Oprah claims to be very "open-minded," she really is closed-minded in some ways. What are some clear examples that Avatari makes reference to? Can you think of any other examples of things that Oprah is closed-minded to?

5. Avatari gives what she says is a good definition of truth. What is it?

6. Avatari talks about self-defeating statements. What is a self-defeating statement?

7. How would you respond to the following quotations:

   "I can't speak a word of English."

   "People can't know any truth about reality."

   "All of our words are useless and meaningless."

   "People shouldn't be imposing their beliefs on others."

   "There is no absolute truth!"

   "Judge not!"

8. Maria indicates that there is some doctrine in the beliefs of Oprah and Eckhart. What are some of those doctrines? Do you agree or disagree with these doctrines?

Session III: Chapters 6–7

1. Have you read Rhonda Byrne's book, *The Secret?* If so, give examples where you agree or disagree with the teachings.

2. In *The Secret,* the reader is supposed to declare, "I think perfect thoughts. I see only perfection. I am perfection." Do you think that this message is consistent with the apostle Paul's teaching on sin?

3. Do you think God could ever use suffering for good purposes in the end? Why or why not?

4. How does Avatari define pantheism? How does it differ from theism?

5. What are some quotations that indicate that Rhonda Byrne, Oprah Winfrey, and Eckhart Tolle hold to some form of pantheistic thought? Can you think of any other popular proponents of pantheistic religions, such as celebrities or movies?

6. Avatari shares that some of the philosophy of Norman Geisler helped her to understand that pantheism was self-defeating. What was the example that Geisler gave?

7. Avatari quoted C. S. Lewis suggesting some reasons why pantheism has been so popular for thousands of years. What did he say?

Session IV: Chapters 8–9

1. Avatari said she felt lonely and abandoned by her family for following Jesus. Has following Christ ever made you feel abandoned by anyone? What happened and what did you do?

2. What got Avatari's attention in believing that the God of the Bible was the real God?

3. Oprah's spiritual teachers Eckhart Tolle and Marianne Williamson say that sin is an illusion. What are some of the logical problems with this idea?

4. If every law has a lawgiver, why does it make more sense that God is the one who determines moral laws rather than people or societies?

5. Read Romans 2:14–16. What does this verse indicate about *natural law* (the objective moral law revealed apart from the Scriptures)?

6. The apostle Paul wrote in 1 Corinthians 1 that Christ's death on the cross was "stumbling block to the Jews" and "foolishness to the Greeks." Even though the spiritual teachers that Oprah Winfrey recommends think that Christ's death is foolishness, why does the Christian faith say that it was necessary?

7. Avatari admitted that she wanted to know Jesus not only as some distant ancient religious guy, but as a real person in history who overcame death. Do you know Jesus personally (not just know *about* him)? If so, when did you come to know him?

DISCUSSION QUESTIONS

Session V: Chapters 10–11

1. What specifically do you believe about the afterlife?

2. Do we have any evidence for an afterlife?

3. What are some of the evidences that Jesus died on the cross historically?

4. Lindsey says many members of weird cults have died for a lie. What's so unique about Jesus' followers dying for their beliefs?

5. Christians are definitely not perfect and sometimes they are inconsistent. In your own personal life, what are some things that you can do to grow in your relationship with Jesus?

6. Sometimes it's difficult for us to forgive. Lindsey and Avatari had to forgive their parents. Have you forgiven everybody that you need to forgive? Have you received God's forgiveness?

7. Have your beliefs about Oprah Winfrey's spirituality changed through reading this book? Why or why not?

8. Should Christians watch "Oprah"? Explain your view.

9. Do you spend more time watching "Oprah" or reading good books exploring the Christian faith? Something to consider: Will you take up the "Read 10 pages a day" challenge? If you miss a day, you don't have to try to read 20 pages the next day. Each day is a new day! If you reach your goal five out of every six days a year, that's 3,000 pages (a least a dozen books) that you will complete in a year! If you have never read the entire Bible, you should start there. Reading the Gospels in the New Testament is a good place to begin. If

you want to know more about true spirituality, or if you still have unanswered questions about the Christian faith, we can recommend these additional books as starters:

Why Trust Jesus, by Dave Sterrett

More Than a Carpenter, by Josh McDowell and Sean McDowell

The Case for Faith, by Lee Strobel

Who Made God (and Answers to Over 100 Other Questions of Faith) by Ravi Zacharias and Norman Geisler

Jesus said, "Keep on seeking and you will find..."[112] We are convinced that if you are a true seeker who is willing to read, pursue truth, and consider the real Jesus, you will not only find satisfying answers to your life questions, but you will likely discover the forgiveness and inner peace you have always longed for.

Endnotes

1. Cathy Lynn Grossma, *USA Today*, "More Americans Dropping Dogma for Spirituality."
2. Ibid.
3. Ibid.
4. Ibid.
5. Ibid.
6. Ibid.
7. Example adapted from Oprah's Angel Network posted on www.oprah.com/entity/angelnetwork or www.oprahsangelnetwork.org.
8. This quote is taken from Oprah and Eckhart's online class. The link can be found under her "Book Club" section posted on www.oprah.com/article/oprahsbookclub/anewearth/20080130_obc_webcast_watchnow.
9. Ibid.
10. Ibid.
11. Eckhart Tolle, *The Power of Now* (Vancouver, B.C.: Namaste Publishing, 1999), 165.
12. 1 John 4:10.
13. Psalm 147:5 (The Amplified Bible).
14. Matthew 10:30.
15. *O, The Oprah Magazine*, vol. 9, number 5, May 2008.
16. Ibid.
17. Ibid., 43.
18. Martha Sherrill, "Welcome to the Banquet," *O, The Oprah Magazine*, vol. 9, number 5, May 2008, 280.
19. Ibid.
20. Ibid., 281.
21. Oprah Winfrey, the first A New Earth Web seminar, March 3, 2008, at www.oprah.com.
22. *O, The Oprah Magazine*, vol. 9, number 5, May 2008, 281.
23. Oprah Winfrey quoted in video clip posted on multiple sites, including www.jesus-is-savior.com/Wolves/oprah-fool.htm.

24. Ibid.

25. Ibid.

26. Acts 4:12.

27. John 14:6.

28. Paul Copan, *True for You, But Not for Me* (Minneapolis, MN: Bethany House, 1998), 73.

29. Martha Sherrill, "Welcome to the Banquet," *O, The Oprah Magazine*, vol. 9, number 5, May 2008, 281.

30. Adapted from Copan, *True for You*, 77.

31. Eckhart Tolle, *A New Earth* (New York: Plume, 2006),17.

32. Richard Abanes, *A New Earth, An Old Deception* (Minneapolis, MN: Bethany House, 2008), 28.

33. James 1:27.

34. Copan, *True for You*, 73.

35. Tolle, *A New Earth*, 70.

36. Oprah Winfrey, the first A New Earth Web seminar, March 3, 2008, at www.oprah.com.

37. Tolle, *A New Earth*, 71.

38. Ibid.,71.

39. *O, The Oprah Magazine*, vol. 9, number 5, May 2008. p. 198.

40. Ibid., p. 284.

41. Martha Beck, "Blinded by the Light," *O, The Oprah Magazine*, vol. 9, number 5, May 2008.

42. John 8:32.

43. Copan, *True for You*, 18.

44. Norman L. Geisler and Frank Turek, *I Don't Have Enough Faith to Be an Atheist* (Wheaton, IL: Crossway Books, 2004), 37–38.

45. This illustration was given by Ravi Zacharias and was quoted in Geisler and Turek's *I Don't Have Enough Faith to Be an Atheist*, 64–65. For more information about Ravi Zacharias's ministry, we highly recommend you to go to www.rzim.org.

46. Tolle, *A New Earth*, 19.

47. Ibid., 25 (emphasis added).

48. Ibid. (emphasis added).

49. 2 Timothy 4:1–4 (HCSB).

50. Rhonda Byrne, *The Secret* (New York: Atria Books, 2006), 128–29.

51. Ibid., 132–33.

52. Ibid., 130.

53. Ibid., 131.

54. Romans 8:18.

55. Philippians 1:21 (emphasis added).

56. Philippians 4:11b–14 (emphasis added).

57. Byrne, *The Secret*, 162.

58. Marianne Williamson, *A Course in Miracles*, lesson 1, found on "Oprah and Friends" Radio posted on www.oprah.com/article/oprahradio/mwilliamson/ mwilliamson_20080101.

59. Ibid.

60. Ibid., lesson 29.

61. Ibid., lesson 70.

62. Psalm 22:1.

63. Psalm 139:7–10.

64. Dr. Noman L. Geisler, *Baker Encyclopedia of Christian Apologetics* (Grand Rapids, MI: Baker Books, 1999), 580.

65. Ibid.

66. David K. Clark and Norman L. Geisler, *Apologetics in the New Age* (Grand Rapids, MI: Baker Book House, 1990), 13.

67. Ibid.

68. Ibid.

69. Kathy Freston, *Quantum Wellness* (New York: Weinstein Books, 2008), 182.

70. Genesis 3:4.

71. R. C. Sproul, *Now That's a Good Question!* (Wheaton, IL: Tyndale Publishers, 1996), 14. Quoted by Alex McFarland in *The 10 Most Common Objections to Christianity* (Ventura, CA: Regal Books, 2007), 22.

72. Psalm 50:21.

73. Philippians 2:9–11.

74. Deepak Chopra, *The Third Jesus* (New York: Harmony, 2008), 212.

75. Byrne, *The Secret*, 162.

76. C. S. Lewis, *Miracles* (New York: Macmillan, 1947), 84. Quoted by Clark and Geisler in *Apologetics in the New Age*, 11–12.

77. Ibid.

78. Matthew 18:3–5 (paraphrased).

79. Proverbs 28:26.

80. Ephesians 2:10 (JB).

81. Ephesians 2:10 (NLT).

82. Psalm 51:13–14.

83. John 7:37–38.

84. Radhakrishnan quote posted on multiple sites including www.nushindusociety.org/test/index.php?topic=66.0.

85. Plato, Theatetus, 152, act 1.

86. This response of Professor Tanaka is adapted from J. Budziszewski, *Written on the Heart* (Downers Grove, IL: InterVarsity Press, 1997), 65.

87. The response of Professor Tanaka is adapted from J. Budziszewski, *How to Stay a Christian in College* (Colorado Springs: NavPress, 2004), 16–17. Please note that Professor Tanaka does *not* symbolically represent J. Budzeszewski.

88. C. S. Lewis, *Mere Christianity* (San Francisco: HarperCollins Publishers, 2001), 6–7.

89. Ibid.

90. Ibid., 41.

91. Tolle, *A New Earth*, 196.

92. Ibid., 22.

93. Romans 2:14–15.

94. Marianne Williamson, *A Return to Love* (New York: HarperCollins Publishers, 1992), 297.

95. *A Course in Miracles* (Mill Valley, CA: The Foundation for Inner Peace, 2007), 380.

96. Colossians 1:17.

97. John 8:58.

98. John 8:59.

99. Geisler and Turek, *I Don't Have Enough Faith to Be an Atheist*, 222–23.

100. Romans 6:23.

101. John 3:16.

102. Dinesh D'Souza, *What's So Great About Christianity?* (Washington, DC: Regnery Publishing, 2007), 286.

103. Ibid., 288–89.

104. Williamson, *A Return to Love*, 297.

105. John 11:25.

106. Gary R. Habermas and Michael R. Licona, *The Case for the Resurrection* (Grand Rapids, MI: Kregel, 2004), 100.

107. Ibid., 49.

108. Paul Copan and Ronald K. Tacelli, eds., *Jesus' Resurrection: Fact or Figment? A Debate Between William Lane Craig and Gerd Lüdemann* (Downers Grove, IL: Intervarsity Press, 2000), 10.

109. 1 Corinthians 15:6.

110. Geisler and Turek, *I Don't Have Enough Faith to Be an Atheist*, 275.

111. 1 Corinthians 15:17–19 (paraphrased).

112. Matthew 7:7 (The Message).